It's been a long journey and Steve and Phil would like to thank:

Peter Wilson for starting the car.
Gerard O'Farrell for tuning the engine.
Vaughan and Gwen Pearce for filling it up and finding the right maps.
Rob O'Connor for the exceptional bodywork.
David Oddy for the tools in the back.

And you lot for letting us come to visit.

A VISUAL HISTORY OF No SECRETS SHOW OF HANDS

Flood Gallery Publishing
3 Greenwich Quay, Clarence Road, London SE8 3EY
www.thefloodgallery.com

First published in 2017 by Flood Gallery Publishing
Copyright ©2017 Show of Hands under sole license to Flood Gallery Publishing
All Stylorouge artworks reproduced remain copyright of Stylorouge Ltd.

Text copyright ©2017 Phil Beer/Alexis Bowater/Elizabeth Kinder/Steve Knightley

Book edited and designed by Stylorouge; Jamie Gibson, Mark Higenbottam, Rob O'Connor
With thanks to Vaughan & Gwen Pearce, Vicky Whitlock, Brad Waters,
Will Johnson, Jane Brace and Bobbie Coppen
and everyone who has so generously helped in the production of this book.
Production coordination by Deborah Pike

Printed in Italy
British Library Cataloguing in Publication data.
A catalogue record for this book is available from the British Library

Deluxe edition ISBN 978-1-911374-01-5

CONTENTS

"From the hole to the hall"

AN INTRODUCTION

On the 16th April 2017, Show of Hands returned to the Royal Albert Hall in celebration of their extraordinary 25 years together. This, their fifth sell-out performance at the landmark venue also marked 21 years since their audacious debut there - when as an 'unknown pub duo', they were struggling to get any London gigs at all. Exceeding all their expectations of success, it spawned a best-selling live album, Show of Hands Live At The Albert Hall (1996) and set the tone for their subsequent career. Going on to headline major festivals the world over, they would also storm bastions of culture closer to home, from the Royal Festival Hall to Shakespeare's Globe and the Glastonbury festival.

So how did Show of Hands, from inauspicious beginnings as a casual duo, become inspirational icons to musicians and fans the world over? In the following pages Knightley and Beer reveal with typical witty understatement how – with a pioneering unconventional approach, an exuberant 'do it yourself, can do' attitude, a very special relationship with your audience and more than 'a little help from your friends' – you can make the soundtrack to people's lives - and the wildest of dreams come true.

Right: An early gig in Hampshire
Opposite: Ticket for the first ever Show of Hands Royal Albert Hall show. Phil and Steve on stage at the Royal Albert Hall in 2001

"The funniest part of it" says Gerard O'Farrell, Show of Hands manager at the time, "was that the guy who ran the Royal Albert Hall – he clearly thought we had no clue whatsoever. Even up to the night, as thousands arrived, he was firmly convinced we were a pack of idiots. I am sure we changed his life, just a little bit."

In the Winter of '94/'95 Show of Hands were trudging up to London, playing here and there – the occasional Sunday night upstairs at Ronnie Scott's, the Irish Centre in Hammersmith, the Half Moon at Putney, but it wasn't picking up. Just after another show where the promoter took the lion's share of the money, Knightley and Beer despaired of ever finding a good gig in the capital. Driving through Hyde Park with their friend Jon Roseman, a showbiz agent and video producer, they passed by the Albert Hall. Knightley voiced his thoughts: "I wonder how much that is to hire?" He was simply musing and it could have ended there. But Roseman replied "I don't know. Let's find out!"

"Roseman discovered it cost 'about twelve grand' a night." With this, the idea though far-fetched, became concrete. First, they'd need a backer. Happily their friend Richard Patterson also happened to be a successful software designer. Pitching their outlandish plan to him, the pair found they weren't laughed out of his house. Patterson said: "If you can get a professional festival organiser on board, I'm in!" The only player Knightley and Beer knew on the folk scene with the relevant experience and expertise was Steve Heap, who organised Towersey and Sidmouth Festivals. So Show of Hands took the trip to Aylesbury and the offices of Heap's company Mrs. Casey Music. Here, having outlined the hall's fee, Patterson's potential involvement and the fact that they had a mailing list naming nearly three thousand people keen to be updated re: their gigs, Beer and Knightley wondered, 'would Heap take up the challenge?' "Bearing in mind" added Beer, "that you can't charge more than a fiver for a folk gig!"

"Well," said Heap, "You've got the sausage - I mean, the music and the mailing list - now we need the 'sizzle'!", and agreed to co-fund the venture with Patterson. But in a stubbornly sizzle-free run-up to the gig their money did not look safe. The first day's ticket sales totalled twelve. No one cared about the story of two West Country folkies going from playing the tiny Albert Hole pub in Bristol to the Albert Hall. Then

This page: Major theatre appearances by Show of Hands and their guests, including Martyn Joseph, Tom Robinson, Port Isaac Fisherman's Friends, Jackie Oates and Emily Sanders

SHOW OF HANDS
TENTH ANNIVERSARY CONCERT

ROYAL ALBERT HALL
SATURDAY 7th APRIL 2001

Judy Totton, a publicist friend of Knightley's, got cooking on gas. In a media coup that suggested Beer and Knightley were risking their homes to realise their dream, that they were in fact bussing the countryside up to London to keep a roof over their heads, she secured mainstream coverage. And, inspired by the idea that they could help make this madcap scheme work, people began buying tickets in droves.

Richard & Judy then enjoying huge nationwide ratings with their morning TV slot sent a producer down from Manchester to film the despair of a 'couple of pub singers' sitting outside the capital's iconic music venue. The musicians were to rue their hubris and impending homelessness due to their insane stab at stardom. "On the Friday before the gig the producer wanted the local film crew to shoot one of us coming out of the hall as if we'd just bought a ticket then to walk down the steps and say: 'so, only another four thousand four hundred and ninety to go'. We said 'can't we say 'that's five thousand sold?' which was nearer the truth. Luckily the hard bitten crew thought the idea was naff and stood up for us - 'tell him to f*** off" said the cameraman' but the idea of two pub singers out of their depth still stuck."

Mrs. Casey Music organised the ticketing, the catering, the security and the coaches for the fans who would make the journey to SW7 from across the country. HZ in Shepton Mallet provided the sound system, which worked perfectly at the local discos for which it was designed. This meant nothing to the management at the Royal Albert Hall. Noting the non-arrival of giant flight-cases containing the usual

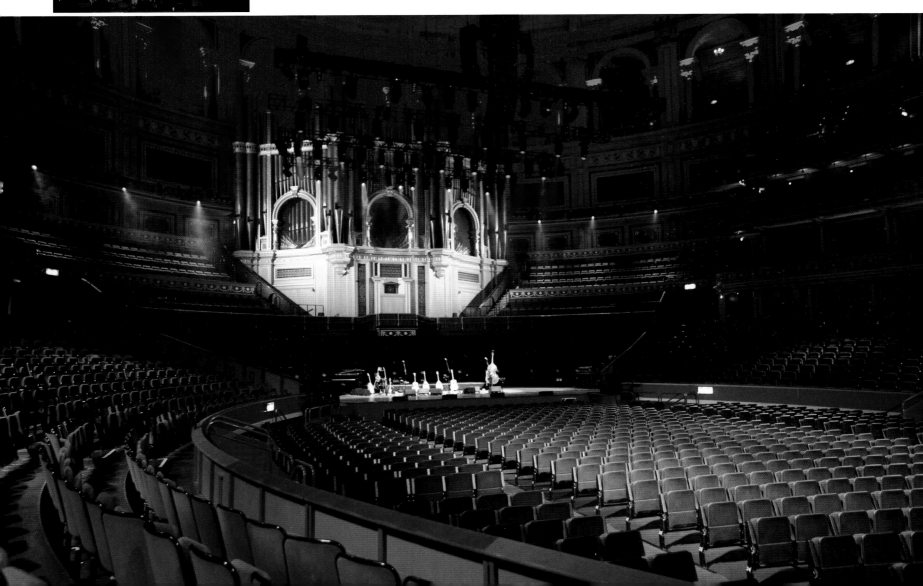

Opposite, top to bottom:
Show of Hands at The Royal Albert Hall
(2001), Vaughan Pearce backstage (2007),
Merchandise from the tenth anniversary
show in 2001, The crew and guests from
the 2007 Royal Albert Hall show.
Interior shot during lighting setup (2012).
This page, left to right, top to bottom:
Artists who have appeared with Show of
Hands at The Royal Albert Hall include:
Matt Clifford, Gareth Turner, Martyn Joseph,
Paul Downes, Sally Barker, Tom Palmer,
Polly Bolton, Vladimir Vega, Ralph McTell,
John Watcham, Tom Robinson,
Albion Morris, Steve, Phil and Miranda
during shows and soundchecks, Port Isaac's
Fisherman's Friends.
Below: John Evans, Paul Downes
and Steve, the original Gawain line-up in the
backstage bar at the Royal Albert Hall
Lower-right: Paperwork regarding the first
ever Albert Hall show in 1996

STEVE: *"For the first Albert Hall show my family were all there, Paul and Bat from 'Gawain' were there, the guys I had started playing with. It was slightly strange in that we'd had an awful lot of publicity but as a pub duo risking everything for stardom. There was Sky News on stage at 5 past 6. We had an awful lot of profile, but it was just in a way 'let's see if these guys fail'... We were told ten minutes before we were about to go on that the amplifiers had broken and we may not have a PA, and we would only know when we went out there and started singing whether the out-front amplifiers were on; they'd tripped down in the cellar somewhere. And it was only when we heard the guy introducing us that we knew the PA was working, so that was nerve-wracking."*

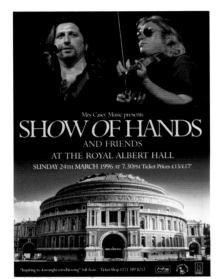

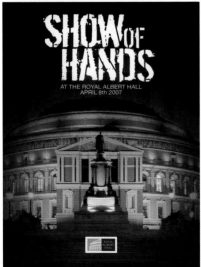

Above: Poster for the first Royal Albert Hall appearance, Brochure for the 2007 show, *Right:* Steve and Phil take a bow, 1996

equipment, RAH staff took O'Farrell aside and aired their growing concerns about his sanity. "There were serious discussions about the absence of the usual rock'n'roll PA, and the discovery we were going to hold a raffle simply cemented the feeling at the RAH that they were dealing with a bunch of West Country yokels."

That Devon instrument maker David Oddy produced a beautiful handmade mandocello for the first prize mattered not to the RAH, nor that the raffle organised by one time fan, now friend Steve Sheldon, was at the heart of the communal folk club feeling that would underpin the night's success. A warm, inclusive feeling that was heightened by the guest appearances of local musicians whom Beer and Knightley had met on their travels, who all pitched up on a flood of goodwill to help make this bonkers debut an unforgettable night.

Then suddenly, just before show-time, disaster almost struck. There was no sound. But before the RAH could say "Told you so!" Mark Greenaway one of the roadies, (Beer and Knightley's mates from the Forest of Dean) crawled under the stage, found the amp that had short circuited and fixed it. So it was just a few minutes later than advertised, that on 24th March 1996 Show of Hands took to the stage to a roar of approval in a sold out venue, that for the first time became known as Kensington's Village Hall.

That first performance at the RAH set the tone for Show of Hands' subsequent sell-out appearances there, all further celebrations to mark notable anniversaries. A roll-call of folk's finest would continue to appear as surprise guests and of course there'd always be a raffle. Ralph McTell appeared at the next gig in 2001 to mark Show of Hands 10th birthday (since Beer left the Albion Band to concentrate on the duo with Knightley), as did Fisherman's Friends - making their first major public appearance. This time media coverage included a multi-camera video shoot. Knightley had just filmed a documentary for Carlton TV in which he travelled the county talking with local craftsmen to write a song about the experience. He was to perform this at his journey's end. This he did as part of Show of Hands set on the upper deck of The Phoenix, a 3-masted ship that had sailed to Topsham on the high Spring tide. On hearing about the planned RAH gig, the programme's producer promptly organised the filming of the event and a 'two-part special' went out on the ITV network. Viewers witnessed Knightley's marriage proposal to his then girlfriend Clare from where he stood on stage. "I'll think about it!" she said. Knightley in an aside to Beer said "Sorry about that." "You will be!" he replied. Knightley may have been taking a chance on love, (though having thought about it Clare said "yes!") but he was not taking one on Show of Hands. With this first return to the Royal Albert Hall, they were "no longer a novelty act taking a punt."

In all of Show of Hands' travels across the globe, perhaps their most extraordinary journey is the four short miles that first transformed their Sunday night London gigs: the journey that took them from the Half Moon pub in Putney to Prince Albert's grand auditorium in Kensington Gore. So it's fitting that their trailblazing, inspirational and unconventional approach was celebrated here, where 21 years ago an impossible dream became brilliant, uplifting reality.

"That first one was nerve-wracking but then we realised that everybody there was there to make it work. We weren't playing to a London audience that had come to check us out, it was our village hall audience all in one place. They'd come from all over the country, they'd been organising buses and coaches and overnight trips...
...As soon as you step out you realise this isn't a crowd that you need to win over, they are your friends, because you can see them in the front row, those people from those folk clubs in those village halls from all over the country...
...Well we knew they would be there, but until you actually get in front of the audience you don't quite know what sort of organism they're going to be. But we treated it like a village hall in a way, by having a raffle. We raffled one of David's instruments which we do every time. So we can't repeat that anxiety of the first one because it's worked four times since."

Richard Shindell with Steve and Miranda.
"Show of Hands has been enormously kind to me - asking me to share their stage (including a previous Albert Hall gala), providing hospitality and shelter when I was vagabonding around the UK, and introducing me to their families and community. So how could I say no when over breakfast one morning they asked to video me trying Marmite for the first time? However they choose to deploy the footage, it's a small price to pay."

STEVE: *"It's a pivotal moment. It's a moment when all that affirmation you've been seeking all your life becomes public. I'm not always particularly proud of the bit of me that needs all that, it's like things like the folk awards, and all that, I wish I could be as indifferent to it as Phil. But behind the scenes, as Phil knows, there's a lot that goes into putting these shows on and constructing the set, I will be planning the set list and the idea of the show inside for months."*

In 2017 Show of Hands took to the Royal Albert Hall stage for the fifth time. Their previous appearance there, in 2012 set new standards in production for a folk act

PHIL ON THE ROYAL ALBERT HALL: *"It's terrific to walk out on that stage. Eric Clapton's played there so many times, so I was just searching for his plectrum. Or Dame Clara Butt's fag end. Dame Clara Butt would have sung there in 1910 a lot. It was great. Obviously it's iconic. It was a bit of a stunt when we did it the first time but we got away with it. Then subsequently, having done it once, it became easier each time...*
I don't prepare, there's no preparation, it's a gig. There's no thought process going on. It's slightly larger than some other gigs, but for me now there's a sense of ownership, I know this place really well, I know where everything is. Of course I've subsequently been there lots and lots of times, not just for our gigs but for things like folk awards and loads of other things. The only thing I've never done is gone to someone else's gig there, I must do that sometime. It is a great place."

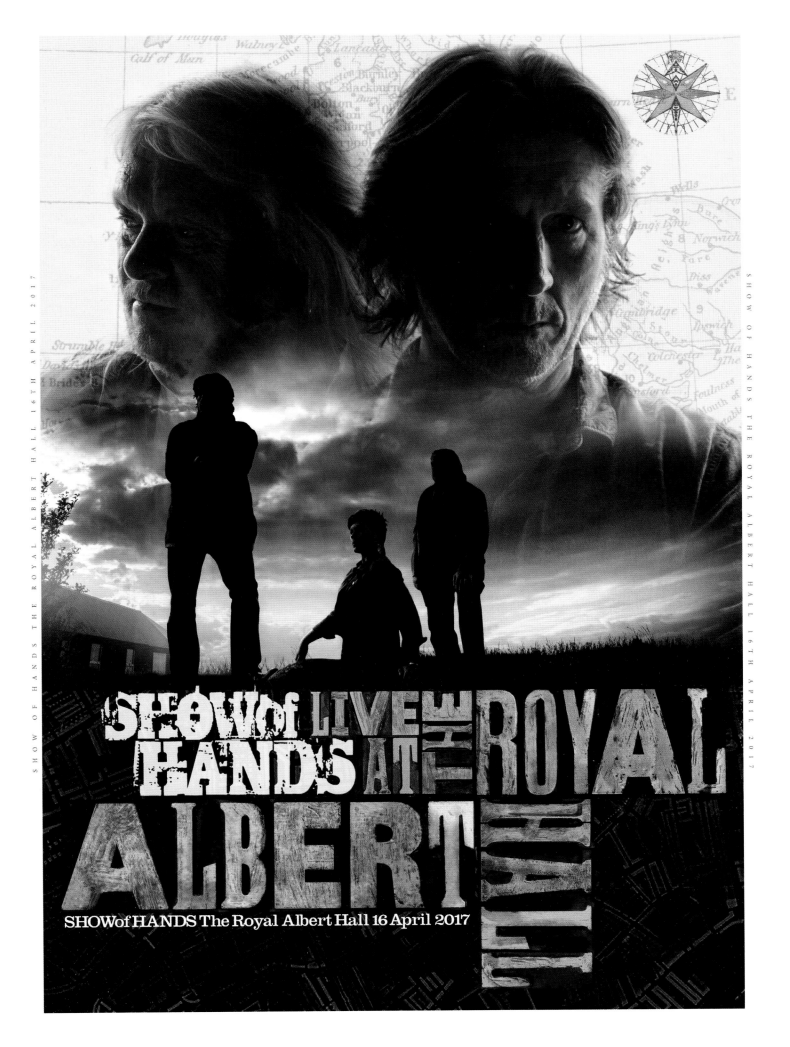

SHOWof HANDS LIVE AT THE ROYAL ALBERT HALL

SHOWof HANDS The Royal Albert Hall 16 April 2017

PHIL: *"Being outside the city boundary, we had to go to the county schools. So Teignmouth was there, 12 miles away, and I was kind of looking forward to that because we would get a train ride every day, and it's a spectacular train ride... To this day, when I've got friends visiting, I'll take them to Exmouth, get on a train and go up the river Exe to Exeter, turn around and then go down to Dawlish and you see the west side of the Exe; you go across all the Brunel stuff, all the stuff that's falling into the sea, finish up in Newton Abbot, go and have a cup of tea in what was the transport café there, then about turn and do it all again. So you get to go up one*

...My father was a pillar of the community and he was Chairman of the Parish Council for a good 30 years of his life. Ultimately, after retiring from his job as one of the senior admins at Exminster Psychiatric Hospital, he was the Chairman of Teignbridge District Council and amongst other things he oversaw all sorts of local things like the connection of the RSPB with the Exminster marshes and so on...

...we were always walking on the marshes. My father was a twitcher and later in life became a not-bad photographer and had his political involvement in the RSPB, getting conservation control of the Exminster marshes. It's a huge bird reserve now."

"Can you see what the future holds?"

STEVE: *"I was not very confident when I was fourteen/fifteen though all my friends seemed to be effortlessly at ease with girls. Every year there'd be about a thousand Summer students studying English as a foreign language, Scandinavians and Germans who wanted music at beach parties and barbeques... One particular favourite was Needle of Death, a Bert Jansch song about a heroin addict. They used to say (Swedish accent) I love Needle of Death, it's so gloomy!"*

Top: Steve as a teenager
Below: a young Phil Beer with
sisters, Phil's parents, Madge and Ken.
Opposite, top left to right
Phil's father played in a number of bands,
seen here left of centre with fiddle.
Phil as a baby with Mother in the garden,
and right as a teenager.

Gloomy, but great news to Knightley. Just sixteen, he was finding that the previous two years spent in his room learning guitar and methodically working his way through the Penguin Book of English Folk Songs were finally paying off: as were the countless hours he'd put in listening to Martin Carthy and this transformative record his neighbour Brian had lent him, The Freewheelin' Bob Dylan. For down at the Devon shore young Knightley discovered that his singing and guitar playing gave him a golden ticket to party time - and a sense of connection with the wider world.

It was around this time that fellow Devon teenager Phil Beer was becoming a bit bored with the violin. He'd taken it up after learning the ukulele from the age of six, inspired (though not taught) by his father, who played the fiddle in local dance bands. These in turn were inspired by Victor Sylvester, the Kingston Trio and the Christy Minstrels whose music played on the radio tuned to the BBC Light Programme that both Beer's parents loved. They'd soak up its staple of commercial American Folk.

Both mum and dad belonged to a local progressive Methodist congregation where music was an integral part of life. His mum played the organ in chapel until she died – and it was singing here, from a quasi religious song book entitled Faith, Hope And Clarity, that her eldest son Philip became intimate with songs by Leon Rosselson and Sydney Carter and others connected with the folk scene.

Yet it wasn't until Beer later became part of that scene himself, that he realised his connection with folk was intertwined with his childhood. And it was later still, as Beer was sadly going through his father's effects, that the depth of that connection was revealed. For finding an old 1910 Scottish songbook full of tunes his father played for him when Beer was small, he suddenly recognised these as the very tunes he loved on albums by Fairport Convention.

PHIL: *"Despite the fact that my dad was a fiddle player and my mum was a piano/organ player, I was actually given a ukulele which I still have, which I was given by an elderly next door neighbour when I was 6, so I learnt to play that, and it's utterly logical that if you learn to play the ukulele that's your step to the guitar, that's where it goes…*

…There was a music shop in Exeter run by a wonderful Jewish guy call Bill Greenhalgh. He had the shop at the bottom of town, and that was the Aladdin's cave of guitars, and amplifiers, and all that kind of stuff. Back in those days you never had the £30 or £40 to buy a semi-decent guitar, but he would look you up and down and if he liked the look of you he would give you a little hire purchase book. He did that for me. You paid your tenner down and you would go in every Saturday subsequently on the bus with your little book and you'd be paying another £2, whatever, down on the thing and he would mark it off, and so on. He would always part-exchange your guitar for a slightly better one. That's how it worked. It's incredible…

…The moment I heard Davy Graham's 'Folk, Blues and Beyond' I thought 'What is that?!!' Despite all the pop music, all the electric music, everything that we were listening to at the time, I thought yes, OK, I get it. I was listening to this album and even though I didn't know anything about eastern music at all I knew that it had eastern undertones to it, and lyrically it's obviously some form of R&B. I got my copy of that album, I learnt every song and to this day I play songs from that album…

…I also started playing the mandolin and the fiddle, for a very specific reason: I got to hear a Fairport Convention album called Full House…. the most extraordinary sound, the swaggering electric fiddle on the opening bars of Sir Patrick Spens where Dave Swarbrick absolutely puts his stamp on the foreground of the music… So I picked up the fiddle and started messing around with it. Dad also wanted another instrument to play and he suddenly discovered that the mandolin is tuned in exactly the same way as the fiddle - G D A E - so my father introduced a mandolin to the house and that also helped. I think he probably didn't see it again once I'd got my hands on it. So now I was playing the guitar and scraping away on the fiddle and playing the mandolin. Then of course more people wanted to play with me, because everyone plays the guitar, but not so many people play the fiddle and mandolin."

STEVE: *"I was 14 years old living in a little seaside town. I played a little bit of guitar but I didn't really quite know what to sing. I'd learned some Hendrix and used to play a bit of Deep Purple. Basically I was strumming in the classroom with a few friends, particularly my older friend, Paul Downes, who's a year older than me, who is a brilliant classical guitarist. But I did know a lot of folk songs from the records that my stepbrother brought home. Like a lot of soldiers they were very much into folk music."*

PHIL ON MUSIC: *"It wasn't even a conscious thing, I was just lost to it. That was it. I went into the first two years of Teignmouth Grammar School sailing through everything, getting straight A's, but the moment this started that was it, that was the end. I was elsewhere, I was away with the fairies... There was no goal. There was no coherent focus, there was nothing. You just had to be able to afford the next set of strings that's all...*

...Geographically Teignmouth Grammar School is immediately next door to what was then Teignmouth Secondary Modern School and the two schools are basically on the same campus, only separated by a little piece of woodland, where people met to do all kinds of things which we probably won't mention! And Colin Wilson was the guitar player in his school, and he lived in Teignmouth. It was always likely that we would get it together musically. Eventually we would form the duo Odd Folk ".

It was in 1968 that Beer discovered the local Devon folk scene. From then until about 1975, it was, he says, "astonishing. We could go to something every night of the week whether it was a folk club or something vaguely calling itself a folk club, long before the concept of open mic. nights."

There were the traditional folk song clubs like the Jolly Porter in Exeter, where Nic Jones and Tony Rose would play, and gigs at teacher training colleges and university accoustic music clubs, where the likes of Ralph McTell, Keith Christmas or Colin Scott would appear; and where adds Knightley, "There'd be smokey, dopey, trippy nights with Incredible String Band stuff. The people running those clubs were ten years older than us, they'd left uni. but we were close enough to hang out and party with them. (It's their kids who are the Bellowhead, Lakeman, Rusby generation). It was all there for us, let alone hearing Bowie and Jethro Tull, or going to the Isle Of Wight Festival. It was all there for us to take a bit of everything."

It was with his clique of friends that included Paul Downes (who a year older had handily passed his driving test) that Knightley, on nights off from playing songs to Swedish girls, would travel to the local

folk clubs in Downes' old Morris 1000 van. Here they'd get to play - given an opening floor spot at 8 o'clock.. "They'd say 'do a couple of songs and we'll buy you a pint.' " It was in this milieu of folk and underage-drinking that he first met Beer, for although they'd grown up for most of their lives less than five miles apart, due to a quirk in the catchment area Beer attended school on the other side of the River Exe in Teignmouth.

PHIL: *"I left school because I was in danger of being found out for not doing anything, and I went to work at Exeter University as a computer tech, back in the days when you could simply open the local newspaper on a Friday night and find four pages of jobs for a youth to do."*

STEVE: "*All of a sudden, at the age of 16 and 17, we were getting gigs all over East Devon. We were staying up late, we were drinking, we were meeting girls. Our parents didn't have a clue what we were getting up to, they would have been horrified... The people running the folk clubs at that time were just university graduates, only 10 years older than us. So they were old enough to hang out with and go back and have a smoke with in their flats, so we were quite close to the generation that were running the folk clubs...*
...We were aware that there was a duo from the other side of the river, from Exminster, from Teignmouth, called 'Odd Folk'. Paul and myself and John Evans were like the Oasis of the time and they were more like the Blur. We were very, very arrogant and probably sexist and full of ourselves, and they were very nice. They were the sort of people who would play to everyone's mums, a lot jollier. Colin is very engaging as a performer and they did a lot of comedy stuff. So there was this gentle rivalry between us and 'Odd Folk'."

Opposite: Gawain (Steve Knightley,
Paul Downes and John 'Bat' Evans)
at the Sidmouth Folk Club (circa 1971)
This page: Phil Beer and Colin Wilson,
Odd Folk outside the Double
Locks Hotel, on the Exeter Ship Canal
- where they and Gawain frequently played

"What you are is where you're from"

THE EARLY YEARS

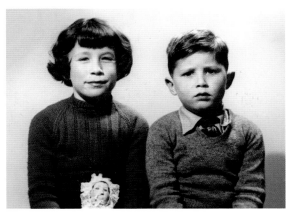

This page, left to right:
Clare, Steve's second wife pictured
with Planxty's Andy Irvine,
Steve Knightley with sister
Christine (1958)
Steve with mother (1954)
Opposite: Steve and family on a
day out at Fishponds Park, Devon,
December 1997. Sister Chris, Steve. Mum
Margaret, step-brother Den, sister Babs, Dad
Philip and brother Dave.

Knightley had gone to school in Exeter aged five and a half when his family moved there from Southampton and then in Exmouth after moving again eight years later. Through soldiers and Royal Marines in his family, young Knightley was immersed in folk music thanks to the thriving folk circuit they experienced in Germany. "You had this strange anomaly of these very tough guys listening to Judy Collins, to Simon & Garfunkel, to Joan Baez in particular and her versions of the Child Ballads. I heard my stepbrother play every Joan Baez album. I saw Martin Carthy at the Sidmouth Folk Festival when I was fifteen and I suddenly understood the connection between what he was playing and the Americanised versions of all these British folk songs. I'd heard all their stuff without realising I had it under my nose at Sidmouth and in the local folk clubs: beautiful old Cecil Sharp collected songs."

STEVE: *"They were from a Southampton family of dockers and soldiers, Dad never had any formal education and he did lots of jobs – he worked for the Social Services for a while in foster homes, some of those awful places that are now in the news, there were resident parents then. He put up aerials, he cleaned carpets, he drove taxis. We moved to Exeter when I was 5. Half of Exeter was a bomb site at that point...*
...That was my environment, Exeter, wandering down to the river through some of the derelict buildings, the tenements that were still deserted. I was always quite solitary; because we moved so much I never grew up with a peer group. I must have moved six times before I was 9...

Other than his father occasionally strumming a guitar or playing an old accordion mostly left lying around, his parents didn't play any instruments and whilst one grandmother hailed from the Scottish Borders and the other from Northern Ireland, they did not knowingly impart any Celtic musical sensibility to their young grandson. His love of Irish music was fired up on first hearing Dublin's Planxty when Knightley was about 19. Coincidentally years later, to his great surprise, Knightley's second wife announced that the group's Andy Irvine is a cousin of hers, though she'd never met him.

...I went to John Stocker, which was a Dickensian junior school, savage in terms of its beatings and the general horror of it. In fact my family were amazed that I had passed my 11+.
...I remember having unrequited love for girls in my year who I was too shy to speak to. I was a bit of a vandal when I look back, I used to break things. I don't think I was angry about anything, it was a loving family, parents were happy, I had brothers and sisters, I had my step-brother. But I just think having moved around so much I didn't have that security of a peer group of friends...
...My kids have grown up with the same friends since nursery school and they're now 15; the same friends. And I quite envy them that security. I never had that."

STEVE: *"Dad used to play the accordion. There was always stuff lying around. There were always pianos in the corner, there was always a guitar. My great uncle somehow left me a 12-string mandolin which I began to gig with. I don't know where these came from but there was nobody playing them seriously. But the house was always full of music, the gramophone was always on. I remember looking at these early Frank Sinatra records when I was about 5, of him in a trilby hat propping up a bar, like one of those Edward Hopper paintings, looking through the glass with a cigarette and a glass of whisky. I remember being really struck by that persona. This is almost pre-Elvis. Sinatra was a huge hero in the house, then Elvis, The Beatles and The Stones took over.*

When we moved to Exmouth, it was one of these new housing estates full of social mobility. There were very, very posh people who were in decline, there were marines all around us, there were young teachers, there were ambitious working class people; and it was party time, from the mid-'70s. My parents used to entertain and drink and carouse a great deal. It was like they came from these working class Victorian back streets of Exeter and St Thomas, to suddenly be in an area where they're surrounded with socially mobile people. We had a big cellar, we used to call it the void, where we used to practise music. Dad put a bar in it and many a night I would just be unable to sleep because they would be down there, drinking and dancing and having fun with the neighbours. I remember that very vividly...

...My step-brother was a colour sergeant in the Royal Green Jackets. And there was a flourishing folk scene in Germany on the bases. Also my brother-in-law was a Royal Marine and it was an odd combination of these very tough guys loving Paul Simon, Judy Collins, Joan Baez, and Bob Dylan. So I heard a lot of his stuff. They used to play Joan Baez records all the time. So I started strumming along to those records and Paul and I gradually realised that there was this folk music genre...

None of us were born into folk-y families like the Lakemans or the Carthys or the Rusbys, it wasn't in our DNA, although I subsequently found that out my grandfather who was a sergeant in the Dorset regiment was a tireless clog and horn-pipe dancer...

...I only really worked at my music. I remember having an argument with one of my teachers who told me I was terminally lazy, saying 'Look, I spend all day long practising the mandolin', and she said 'That doesn't count, that's not the same'. I thought to myself 'I can't be as lazy as I'm being told I am' because I used to practise the mandolin and the guitar for hours... There was this club in Exmouth called the Deer Leap that used to run twice a week and in the Summer the audience was a lot of foreign language students from Scandinavia and Germany between the ages of 15 and 18, very attractive people, can I say, Danes and Swedes. And unlike girls of our own age they would talk to us. Girls of our own age went out with older blokes with cars, that was the way it was. So there was me, a rather awkward, gawky, shy 15 and 16-year old suddenly having people to play to – beach parties and foreign language school barbecues, as well as this folk club.

I always used to visualise being on stage playing: even before I played the guitar I can remember walking down the street with my head full of poses and shapes that I imagined I could see myself doing. But I didn't have any way I could realise that. I still do that now and I didn't realise that this was my approach ."

STEVE: *"...I was three years at Hele's Grammar School in Exeter. I was failing academically and always in a lot of trouble, I wasn't a good pupil, lots of black marks against me. I used to fool around all the time. I hated school. All I loved was fooling around with my friends and the rugby side, the sports side of it. That was the only consolation... My parents didn't even know what O'levels I was taking. I used to forge all my reports. In the book it says "This intelligent young man continues to squander all his time on ill-considered thought and observation". That was me.."*

STEVE: "After a while it becomes the way that you're perceived, within the family and within your peer group you're the guy that plays music. You get invited to parties – 'can you bring your guitar'."
Steve (above) performing in a cabaret show at the Sallis Benney Hall, Brighton Art College

STEVE: "I realised there was, in the English tradition, stuff that was influencing the American music I was hearing. So Paul [Downes] and I got totally obsessed with Martin Carthy and we learned all this stuff".

They may not have been particularly musical but his parents appreciated Knightley's ability to entertain and encouraged his appearances on the local folk circuit as one third of Gawain with Paul Downes and John ('Bat') Evans. The trio — inspired by Martin Carthy & Dave Swarbrick worked up their set from Knightley's dog-eared copy of the Penguin Book Of English Folk Songs whilst also covering Dylan and McTell songs and airing Knightley's own first compositions. And so the young band added audience applause to parental approval — although the idea of their parents actually turning up horrified them. These gigs were their world.

After two years with Gawain, Knightley left East Devon for the Midlands to gain a degree in politics and modern history at Lanchester Polytechnic in Coventry, where he realised his dream of running a folk club like the ones in which he loved to play. It was here that Beer, who by now was playing in a duo with Paul Downes, first met Leon Rosselson when they were all booked to play on the same night. Beer, honing his skills as a multi-instrumentalist and professional musician, was also working with Johnny Coppin, whom he'd met in 1969 when the two were both crashing out on Cornish folk legend Brenda Wootton's floor.

PHIL: *"Paul and I weren't playing with Steve but we were playing one or two of Steve's songs and he was constantly writing, emanating new songs. We were touring constantly in a Morris 1000 Traveller, which is good for the soul but not for the arse! So we move up to Cheltenham because it's central and that proves to be exactly the right thing to do. But Paul ultimately didn't stay in Cheltenham. He and I were doing less and less gigs, and I was doing more stuff with other people.*

I met Johnny Coppin on Brenda Wootton's floor, the then self-proclaimed queen of Cornish folk music, who held court in her house at the end of every gig. Hundreds of people would come back to their house and there would be an endless supply of toast coming out. Because it was the English west coast in the Summer everyone was around: Ralph McTell — all of those itinerant travelling musicians who all, well, they couldn't do Route 66 so the English equivalent was going to Cornwall for the Summer. By the time I moved to Cheltenham it was 1976-7 and I'm in the Johnny Coppin band."

Above: Johnny Coppin
Right, Left to right: Gawain
(John 'Bat' Evans, Steve Knightley
and Paul Downes) supporting
The Groundhogs, Sidmouth

STEVE: *"The Cornish scene was thriving, people like Ralph McTell were down there and Wizz Jones and Bert Jansch. Also the local TV would have an acoustic troubadour, who happened to be hanging around, touring or on their way to Cornwall. They used to give them a little studio spot, always on a Friday night."*

PHIL: *"Lanchester Poly at the time was a political hotbed of junior left-wing people who subsequently went on to have a lot to do with the far left of the Labour party. Knightley was happy to run the folk club and decided to move it to a pub, which was even nicer then, the college folk club in a pub. There were some great nights there... I saw an awful lot of amazing people. There is a stalwart still with us, a political songwriter called Leon Rosselson who was part of the songwriting end of the folk revival – very committed, left-wing politics, extremely powerful songs, utterly full of strong, reasoned social content...*
...We made a bunch of friends at that time in Coventry, pretty much lifelong friends which included Rob O'Connor. Rob did the artwork for my and Paul's second album, 'Dance Without Music'. It was Rob's first album sleeve, it's a hand-drawn picture. Then the rest is just history!"

Top main: Steve with college friend Richard Mills
Top right: Steve, returning to his old Exmouth School common room, playing his uncle's 12-string mandolin (1975)
Bottom, left to right: Steve busking whilst visiting the Isle of Man Folk Festival 1976 where he won a singing competition Student Photobooth shots, a poster from one of Steve and Warwick Downes' performances at Lanchester Poly Folk Club (1976)
Above: 'Dance Without Music' album cover

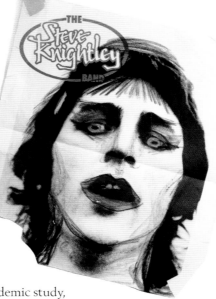

Continuing to weave in work on his songwriting skills with academic study, Knightley decamped to Brighton to win a post-graduate teaching certificate.

STEVE: *"I used to say I was going to join the marines and then I realised if I told anybody I was going to become a teacher they wouldn't ask any more. That was always a good way;'What are you going to do when you're older?','I'm going to be a teacher'. Everyone would shut up then. I never thought I would end up doing it but that was a good way of ending the conversation...*

...I had friends in Brighton and it was party town. It was extraordinary. I went from an environment in Lanchester where it was 8 blokes to every girl, to an environment in Brighton where it was the complete reverse. And by then I was the young, fairly self-confident, if not arrogant, moody singer/songwriter. Yes, well, full of myself. I suppose I had a great sense of entitlement and must have been very opinionated...

I became the blue-eyed boy in Brighton in my early 20s, and a bit of an object of attraction for some of the fragmented relationships amongst that lot. So I had quite a lot of encounters with slightly older women, 5 or 6 years older, who would then take me to task for being an arrogant shit. I can recall a few incidents like that: "Who do you think you are" blah blah blah. Love 'em and leave 'em, I'm afraid I was a bit like that. I was making up for a lot of lost time."

PHIL: *"At that time I'd reached a crossroads, I'm sick to death of the whole thing, as periodically happens to me, I just get sick of being on the road and touring. And a funny little thing happens, I get introduced to a guy called Paul Lindsey and he is Mike Oldfield's studio engineer. I end up hanging out there, staying rather a lot, being in the studio. Michael is at that point in time a strange character...*

This is well after Tubular Bells, by the time I've got there he's beginning to work on a massive thing called 'Incantations'. So I'm around while that's happening and I'm there as a bit of a studio gofer, helping Paul Lindsey in his little tiny technical shop manufacturing bespoke audio analysers and that kind of stuff...

...Michael is getting to this idea where he does actually want to do a serious European or maybe even a world tour of some kind. About 6 months before the big 1979 tour he's recruited a third of the London Symphony Orchestra, and is tending to recruit his other musicians from people he knows. He obviously thought I was an OK guitar player at the time, so he's recruited me and another guitarist called Nico Ramsden and a huge range of astonishing players and people – to play his music. So we start rehearsing all this stuff and I'm really struggling to keep up with some of these players – Pekka Pohjola, a Finnish bass player, astounding, astonishing musicians, Pierre Moerlen from Gong. All these people are dead now, they've all died within the last five years, I don't know why, they're only my age. About two-thirds of the way through rehearsals, Michael literally auditioned two or three other guitar players at the last minute to replace me, all better players than me, but he didn't like any of them as people. So I ended up doing it and once the tour got rolling then it kind of worked. It was actually fine. There were some not-quite-stadium-size gigs but certainly very large arena shows on that... One of them is the biggest indoor arena I've ever been in. We are talking about 30,000 people. Quite big, and it's pretty much full as well. So an extraordinary experience culminating in a tour of London in which we came back and then we went to Wembley. So I had a bit of a taste of the big gigging, big production type thing, and I realised yeah, it's a bit of a laugh, but it's not really for me...

...There's a lot of embarrassing footage out there, including a film shot at the time, and it's available again. I doubt anyone would recognise me now.

...The interesting thing in all of this, Maddy Prior from Steeleye is also on this tour. I'd never met her before and we've been mates for ever since then, which is rather nice."

Above: Record cover for Mike Oldfield's live
album 'Exposed'
Phil in Gloucestershire

STEVE: " I was very jealous. Blimey, when Phil was rehearsing on a barge in London at Mike Oldfield's place and he would say "Come on up to London and hang out' And I'd hang out on this barge and see he was living in a world of transport-to-stadium gigs. By then I'd formed more of a rock band in Brighton, a straightforward rock band in fact, I'd become disaffected with the folk scene, and I was told that with my songs and with my persona I ought to be in a band, shouldn't be wasting time playing folk songs."

Above: Club gig for Paul Downes & Phil Beer
Below: Bill Zorn and Paul Downes ham it up
during an Arizona's show
Right: Arizona Smoke Revue tour schedule

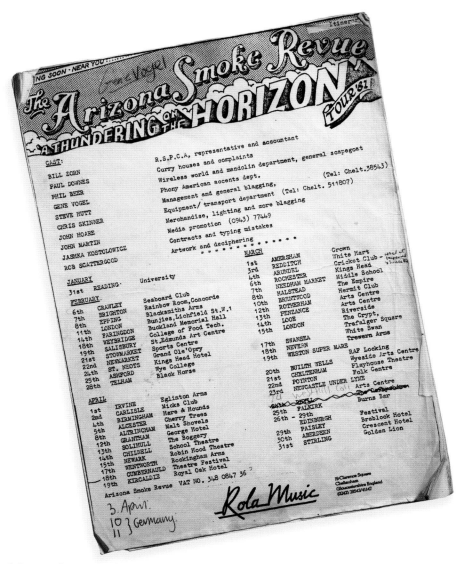

STEVE: *"Phil rejoined Paul Downes and had formed an Anglo-American country folk group called the 'Arizona Smoke Revue' and I used to session with them, but I was under contract and I wasn't allowed to be Steve Knightley. So the leader of the band Bill Zorn said: 'Why don't you be someone else then?'. I said 'OK'. I'd bought this little baseball top and it had G Vogel on it so Bill just looked at it and said 'You're Gene Vogel now.' I said 'Where am I from Bill?'. He said 'You're from Moosejaw Saskatchewan. You ain't going to meet anyone there'. So every night I was introduced as Gene Vogel from Moosejaw, and I didn't have to say anything, just play the bass and nod."*

PHIL: *"We like to think of the Arizona Smoke Revue as a band that was 15 years before its time, I think that's the euphemism we'll use! We had riotously good fun for a very short period of time.*
...So we've got this mad band, it rambles on in a pleasantly pissed and stoned way for a while, largely including myself, Paul Downes, Bill Zorn and Pete Zorn. But this group slightly dissipated, it was kind of banging its head against a brick wall and going round in circles like so many bands because it was impossible to see where it was going to go, and it had an unsympathetic management at the time who thought it should just turn itself into some sort of daft MOR semi-comic thing, which is not really where I saw it going...
...At that time I got the inevitable call from Ashley Hutchings saying 'Hello, would you like to join the Albion Band'. It comes to everyone eventually, we call it the musicians' equivalent of jury service. And lo and behold I reported for duty with the Albion Band. My first gig with the Albions was in Dartington at the Great Hall. It was good fun. There was an interesting career going on then, if you could call it that. It was a very good experience and we managed to do some pretty amazing things over the time."

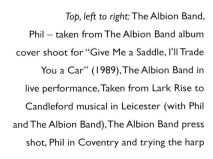

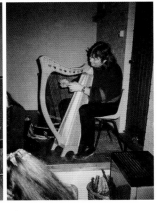

This page, top, left to right: Warwick Downes in his Brighton music shop, Tom Robinson – an early influence for Knightley, Short Stories (Les Maas, Barry Wickens, Steve, John Hoare and Julian Dyke) Above: Steve with Warwick Downes.
Below: Ephemera from the London years
Right: Publicity shot of The Cheats (Les Maas, Neil Waterman, John Hoare and Knightley)
Opposite, top, left to right: Series of shots taken of The Cheats at The Music Machine, Hampstead, London. Steve fronts The Cheats at the Buccaneer, pretentious poster for Total Strangers, New Wave style, hand-made publicity for Short Stories

In Brighton, Steve played in a duo with Paul Downes' brother, bassist Warwick Downes, before heading up to London to make his way on the London pub circuit in pursuit of rock stardom. Turning his back on the narrative lyrics he'd been writing, Knightley now concentrated on 'I love you, need you' type songs whilst supporting himself by teaching guitar at Quintin Kynaston, a tough inner-city comprehensive. "I was writing my own songs, new-wave up-tempo 'shouty' songs inspired by Dire Straits, The Police and the Tom Robinson Band; they were so cool. Tom was a rock star, he's a good friend now. And Squeeze – proper pub bands who'd just left that circuit because they'd been signed."

Knightley landed a management deal with the help of Neil Waterman who worked for EMI publishing and for the next six years found himself plunged into the milieu of the major music business under the wing of Jon Roseman. As well as managing, Roseman was the agent for many of Capital Radio's star DJs, including Nicky Horne and Tommy Vance and had also produced Queen's game-changing video for Bohemian Rhapsody. But it was Waterman who put a group together for Knightley, who stormed the pub rock circuit in three bands, Short Stories, The Cheats and Total Strangers, between 1979 and 1985.

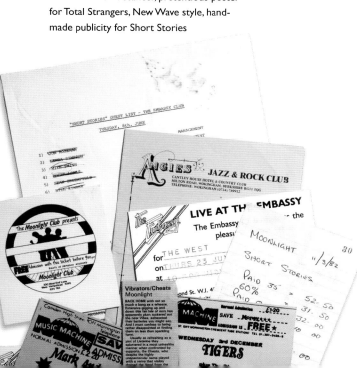

TOTAL STRANGERS

SHORT STORIES

"*You have to be political to run a band really. You have to be aware of everybody's agendas and try and balance them. Sometimes, particularly in London when I was in the rock band, you're the only one who knows the whole picture between agents, managers and all the competing agendas of other musicians, you're at the centre of the spoke, you're the hub. And sometimes you control the information that goes this way and that way, and to a certain extent it's still a bit like that; I'm in the centre of the hub, I probably know the whole picture more than anybody and everyone refers their information through me rather than bilaterally. So you have to become a political animal to do that.*"

STEVE: "*I moved to London, doing the pub scene, doing the rock scene, looking for publishers, looking for deals, looking for managers, that whole world, that whole real predatory world. It was very different to the folk scene. But after a while I began to realise I didn't have quite what it took, I wasn't really that hungry. The guys I met would sacrifice anything and anyone to get on, to get a deal...*

...Even the ones who didn't get anywhere were prepared to sacrifice everything: social life, family life, relationships, anything. The hunger that you see in the hard core rock and roll world, I thought 'Hmm, I'm a bit too grounded for this', I was in a relationship then with Simone who was my first wife, I just didn't want to give it all up. I instinctively knew that I might have had the musical ability but I didn't have the personality. I sensed that really...

...A veteran rock and roller at a party in Brighton told me: 'You'll never make it in London, you're too nice' I said 'I'm going to go and do this', and he just told me 'No way mate' He might have been a major player, he was an older guy in his 40s. He said: 'Don't bother mate, I've only known you 10 minutes, I don't even have to hear you play a note'. I remember that, that rather made a mark.."

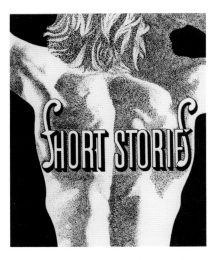

Right: Short Stories (Steve, Les Maas and Barry Wickens shown) playing live at The Cartoon, Croydon
Above: Promotional Sticker designed by Simone Knightley
Below: Phil Beer joins Steve, Albion Band drummer Trevor Foster and BBC sound engineer Miti Adhikari as they steal some down-time at BBC Maida Vale Studios to mix some Short Stories recordings
Opposite: Phil at Cambridge Festival, 1998

STEVE: *"When being a rock star in London hadn't worked out we (his first wife Simone and Steve) sold the house in Maida Vale. February half-term in '86 we just drove around the West Country in a camper van thinking 'Let's pick somewhere to live'... We arrived at Bridport and then I drove inland five or six miles, a little town called Beaminster and thought 'Let's live here'. We just drove around and stayed in the camper van in and around Beaminster, went to a local estate agent and said 'We've got a house in Maida Vale, what can we buy down here?' and he said 'Quite a lot'".*

A year later when Knightley was in his early thirties, his management pulled out. He thought: "I've had a go. I've tried and music hasn't worked out for me. So I moved to the wilds of Dorset with my first wife. It was just north of Bridport, a beautiful area. We had a guest-house. And we put a studio above the garage." Here, he continued to write when he could, but felt frustrated as he wasn't gigging. So when given the chance to put together a line up for the Wimborne Folk Festival in 1986, Knightley jumped at it. "I'd known the Wimborne Festival lot from my old folky days and I put together a trio with Martin Bradley on concertina and my old friend Warwick Downes on double bass. I didn't want it to be 'Steve Knightley' though. I called us Show of Hands. I liked the idea of the democratic implications, the political collective feel of the name." His old mate Beer showed up.

STEVE: *"Phil said 'Look, you've still got all these songs', this was in '86, Why don't I book some folk club gigs, because I know a lot of people in the folk club, I've got some time before I'm touring with the Albion band' or whoever, and God bless him he said 'We'll do some gigs' in 1987. That's 30 years ago this month (January 2017), almost to the day, Phil and I went out touring as a duo, and we kept the name Show of Hands."*

PHIL: *"When Knightley turned up to the Wimborne Festival and played 'Exile', it was a key moment for me, I knew things were going to massively change. I thought that was literally one of the best songs I've ever heard and if he's writing material of that standard that's got to be good...*
...I had already been in the Albion Band a couple of years, very busy, plenty going on, but Knightley is now disillusioned with London life and is wanting to return to the west country in some way shape or form. The following year we were doing stuff together. That moment was a key factor in it all. I've only thought this through in the last five or six years but I realise it's a key factor."

PHIL: *"We were a working item earlier than everyone thinks we were, but I was still in the Albion Band until end 1991, that late. Steve and I were playing regularly together, doing quite a few gigs... I was living the other side of Gloucester by then, in Maisemore. I lived in a sub-manorial farmhouse, massive, literally a small manor house, for about £300 a month. It was falling down, it was genuinely sinking into the pond.*

...The Albion Band meandered its way along quite happily and in 1990 we made an album called 1990. It's a good album but I realised also that the writing was on the wall for the thing and it was time to move on, and the obvious 'thing' for moving on was for Steve and I to formalise the relationship. There literally was this turnover at Christmas and Knightley and I went straight out to our first 70-gig club date tour."

The studio over the garage at Catsley House was at first a rarely visited sanctuary for Knightley. For situated in a local beauty spot a few miles outside picturesque Beaminster, Knightley and his first wife were running their home as a whole-food guest-house. The past seven years on the London rock scene had convinced Knightley he should do something, anything else with his life. He took up teaching history and media studies at the local comprehensive, keeping his hand in playing by teaching guitar. One of his pupils was to realise the rock'n'roll success that eluded him. Pitching up on Knightley's doorstep one day with her then 16 year-old daughter Polly, his neighbour Eva Harvey, asked Knightley if he'd teach Polly the guitar. They struck a genuine countryside 'skills based' agreement. Knightley would supply guitar lessons and her parents, who owned a quarry, would supply him with topsoil and Hamstone in return. Polly bought her first electric guitar - a Stratocaster copy - from Beer and PJ Harvey was off on her stellar musical career. Then in January 1987 Knightley tentatively took up the reigns of his again. 'Catsley House Studio' suddenly saw action as Knightley and Beer set about recording their first album, Show of Hands, Phil making the trip from his new home in Maisemore, Gloucestershire.

The pair were soon playing in pubs and and folk clubs throughout the West Country thanks to the long list of contacts in Beer's little black book. Steve was gig-fit from years of honing his act on the London pub-rock circuit and Beer from his own roots band gigs and as a new signing to the Albion Band.

Used to competing with the darts competition and the sports TV in dockers and bikers pubs from Portsmouth to Plymouth, Beer and Knightley knew how to work to win over their audience. There was no faffing about tuning up between numbers and no jokes off mic. Instead it was direct communication with the punters. Their initial mix of Knightley's original compositions with folk standards and pub favourites gradually morphed over a couple of years into a set list composed entirely of original songs, a selection of which the pair recorded onto cassette to sell at gigs.

Left: Steve and Phil on stage at Cambridge Folk Festival and Phil in Rudolstadt, Germany, early '90's
Bottom: Show of Hands at Corn Exchange, Dorchester, early '90's.
The 'local' pub The Bridge Inn, Topsham

STEVE: "*We just did every gig we could get. Mostly pubs and bars. But because of my London experience, and a 'rock'n'roll' streetwise persona, we didn't dither around. After about two years we'd taken the folk standards out of the set and were playing all original stuff. We were playing loud and quick, and not spending forever tuning up in the pubs. People would be clapping and we'd be 1,2,3 and onto the next one. It was great grounding for festival gigs, but we'd have to tone it down in the folk clubs, where it could be too much.*"

TALL SHIPS

SHOW OF HANDS

STEVE KNIGHTLEY
& PHIL BEER

This page, top: Tall Ships, Show of Hands
third album released on cassette only (and
subsequently re-packaged)
Below: Early Show of Hands gigs,
including (top to bottom) an informal evening
at Arthurs Fish Restaurant, Bridport.
Steve Knightley, Paul Downes and John Bickford
in a re-enactment of the Duke of Monmouth's
visit to Topsham
Opposite top: Phil concentrating during the
recording of their first live album in Bridport
Bottom right: Bridport Arts Centre, 1994

Self-released on cassette only, the duo shifted copies at gigs as they embarked on a sedate round of local clubs on the circuit where they'd first met as young teenagers.

One more 'Catsley House' cassette followed, though not until three years later, partly due to Beer's sudden increase in commitments with the newly reconvened Albion Band. Tall Ships (1990) featured Knightley's 22 minute epic musical suite of the same name on the A side. A composition that he'd worked on with Warwick Downes whilst the two were performing as a duo during Knightley's student days in Brighton, Tall Ships sprang from Knightley's natural talent for taking a folk story to tell a tale. A talent nourished by his childhood beside the sea and his sense of being stranded, left behind once the holidaymakers and students had departed. A deep-rooted and pervasive feeling, it fuelled (and continues to fuel) Knightley's passion for weaving narratives that bring his love of history to vivid, visceral life: stories that supply both boy and man with the excitement that always disappears in the desolation of a seaside resort out-of-season.

Both Show of Hands and Tall Ships sold out and cemented the duo's growing reputation on the local circuit. Seeing that demand for their particular take on the folk tradition was only increasing, Beer opted to leave the Albion Band in 1991 to concentrate on his work with Knightley. This was now flourishing thanks to a meeting with local agent Peter Wilson.

In 1991, needing a new album to sell at their gigs, the pair packed off to The Old Court Studio in Devon to record Out For The Count, which again was released on cassette only and quickly sold out.

This page: Steve and Phil on stage at
Cambridge Folk Festival and Cropredy (above)

1987-92

❖ Show of Hands record their first album which gets a modest self produced cassette-only release. "Show of Hands" is offered for sale mainly to their live audiences

❖ Tall Ships is released, again on cassette It features the 22 minute long title track – a maritime flavoured montage of song and spoken word, with Jim Carter guesting as narrator

❖ Steve and Phil hit the road in earnest playing as many live shows as possible

❖ Recorded between shows, Out For The Count is released, swelling their cassette catalogue to three titles

❖ Show of Hands Live album is recorded at The Bull Hotel in Bridport, documenting a single intimate live show in front of an invited audience. Recorded and produced by Mike Trim, guests include Mike Silver, Paul Downes and Polly Bolton

STEVE: "Realising that music can be life threatening puts it on a different level. This really brought home its power to change things and the possibility of making a difference through writing. It gave us a bit more attitude and focused my writing very much."

música : história : alianza
a unique anglo chilean collaboration

Opposite: Alianza programme and publicity shot. The Anglo-Chilean musical collaboration comprised Knightley, Sergio Avila, Beer, Dave Townsend, Mauricio Venegas and Vladimir Vega

PHIL: *"These guys were exiled in Britain because playing music for them actually turned into a life-threatening situation. As in all fascist states, all public meetings of any way shape or form are banned, including concerts. Plus the fact that a couple of the guys were involved in a rural literacy campaign, which involved music. So you realised that just doing the thing that you're doing blithely and happily in a free country like ours, doing effectively the same thing in somewhere like Chile at the time was a life-threatening thing, and that doesn't half give you a sense of perspective."*

Out of the blue early in 1992 a call came from Roger Watson, who was working at the Southern Arts Development Project (TAPS), seeking to bring folk to a wider audience, partly through inspired collaborations between local and world musicians. "He said he knew three Chilean exiles who wanted to collaborate with English artists, and if it works, there's a tour in it."

Not only did a tour ensue, but also an album, the eponymously titled Alianza (1992), which also featured Dave Townsend on fiddle and concertina. "We were thrown together with these guys our age, Sergio Avila, Mauricio Venegas and Vladimir Vega, who had been imprisoned, tortured and exiled (Vega, a former airforce pilot, for his opposition to the Pinochet regime). Pinochet had banned public meetings - and they were folk musicians running a literacy campaign! They were playing music that sounded like street music, effervescent and rhythmic, totally aware of its power to educate and inform. In our society people can say outrageous things in song and no one will shoot you. But for them, just getting together and playing ordinary songs they risked torture, imprisonment and exile."

Working with the rhythmically driven Chilean musicians, whose percussive way of playing lifted Knightley and Beer's own rhythmic sensibility had a profound impact on the duo. They were inspired to incorporate new instruments such as the cuatro into their repertoire, along with those new rhythms. "It was great to be making that noise, with the drums and charangos and the pan pipes and the horse's jaw!"

The experience served to boost Knightley's musical connection with his social conscience, and songs written at the time such as Santiago, Armadas and Columbus (Didn't Find America) are crowd favourites to this day.

PHIL: *"The influence that they exerted on us is obvious – we still use an instrument called the cuatro, which is a glorified ukulele, a south American small guitar, and we still use it to this day. The song 'Santiago' was written specifically for that project."*

Whilst touring with Alianza, Knightley and Beer kept up the punishing gigging schedule as Show of Hands, and a recording of their June 8th performance at the Bull's Head in Bridport, Show of Hands Live '92, was released to rave reviews. It secured them slots on the following year's festival circuit and crucially, a sixty-date tour with Ralph McTell. McTell, a favourite from their time on the folk circuit as teenagers, took the pair under his wing. "Look guys, you've got to stop doing endless gigs! Call it a tour. Get a concept behind it. Give it a name and have a record that goes with it. Otherwise it'll just be a same old gig. And stop doing free admission! Make it admission only. Group the gigs into touring periods and be self contained."

Whilst giving structural advice and imparting lots of ideas on stagecraft, McTell, having noticed the increasing fan mail and the unnerving, startling persistence of a couple of their female fans said "You need a Suzy."

Opposite: A series of photos taken during the recording of Show of Hands Live '92 album. Guests included Paul Downes, Mike Silver, and Matt Clifford Top left is producer Mike Trim

This page, below: A well-earned aftershow curry for friends and collaborators On the left behind Paul Downes is the bearded Peter Wilson – Show of Hands first booking agent

"Who's Suzy?"

"She's a fictitious female secretary. She's good at writing 'Dear..., Thank you for your kind interest in Steve Knightley's and Phil Beer's career, the demands of which mean they are unable to reply.' Sincerely, Suzy. That should deter the stalkers. If you're going for it, this is what you must do."

Touring with McTell, Show of Hands leapt up another level in their career, winning over a wider audience across the UK as they were playing to large crowds in theatres. Believing now that it saved them two years of hard slog, they took all his advice to heart and conceived an inspired business model that today is held up as an ideal to any musician, aspiring or otherwise. It was only Suzy that had no impact at all.

As the duo exhausted the performing potential initially outlined by Beer's contacts, Bridport based agent Peter Wilson got them gigging hard – particularly to unforgiving audiences in the market towns and resorts along the South Coast. Learning which songs worked best and the delivery to match, Show of Hands built up a strong and loyal following there, that is quite different in its make up to the folk club crowd, for whom they had to tone things down a bit. This in turn differed to the arts centre audience to which they were introduced as they toured Alianza.

SHOW OF HANDS 1993

✤ Tour support for Ralph McTell

✤ Peter Wilson of Peter Wilson Music Management in Bridport takes over gig bookings/management of Show of Hands

COLUMBUS

SHOW OF HANDS

SHP

South Hill Park

the CHESTNUTS

At The Heathcote

Advance Ticket

Date 12/09/93

Artiste SHOW OF HANDS
+
PETE MORTON

Member / Non Member

SHOW OF HANDS
20-Feb-93 at 8pm
TICKET 7 £5.00

McTELL

Summer Festivals 1993
April 10 Gosport 13 Butlins, Bognor Regis May 8 St Neots
15 Portsmouth 15 Brighton June 4,5 Folk, Arts and Cider, Bude
11 Wimborne 13 South Petherton 27 Glastonbury July 18 Larmer Tree, Blandford
25 Trowbridge 31 Cambridge August 3 Sidmouth 5 Guernsey 6 Bridport

Black & White Tour Programme

"If you can't break the mould,

Wasting no time in putting McTell's advice into action, Beer and Knightley decamped to West Dorset and Wytherstone Studios in January (1994). Deciding on Beat About The Bush as the name for the album and the subsequent tour, Beat About The Bush was released on 19th February on Isis Records. Recorded by Mike Trim, who'd delivered success on the live album (and signed the band to his record label), he suggested using a bigger line-up that included a rhythm section. This was, he argued, essential to a radio-friendly album – and securing airplay was the logical next step.

And so the album featured guest appearances from a lot of musician friends: Pete Zorn (bass/ saxophone), Nick France (drums/tea tray), Matt Clifford (piano), Vladimir Vega (vocals/charango/ zamponas), Ralph McTell (vocals/harmonica), Steafan Hannigan (Uilleann pipes and bodhran) and Biddy Blyth (flute/harp/whistle). They all helped the duo to bring to life musically the local stories now fuelling Knightley's songwriting.

break the rules" BUILDING THE BRAND

Left: The 1994 album cover image for
'Beat About the Bush'
Above: Early Royal Albert Hall gigs,
including an appearance with Ralph McTell

For Knightley was finding inspiration from the people he was meeting, farmers, quarrymen, the villagers who worked with their hands on the land. They'd tell him their stories in the local, The Fox in Corscombe, where Knightley played darts and cricket. It was the start of Knightley's way of thinking that brilliantly coalesced on the later Country Life album. Though his storytelling shines too on Beat About The Bush, notably on The Galway Farmer written to replace Kilgerry Mountain in the set. It became an instant Show of Hands classic that would be featured on the Best Of British Folk compilation in 2000. It remains a popular live number and now pops up on websites featuring traditional Irish folk music...

Put together by Peter Wilson, the agent whom the band had met in Bridport in 1991 and who kept Show of Hands busy gigging up and down the South Coast, the Beat About the Bush tour took them further afield. Named for the expanse of travelling in the way one might cross the Australian outback, it took in at least 120 gigs from Land's End to the Scottish borders

The tour featured not the recording band but Knightley and Beer as a duo. So for the first time in Show of Hands' career there was a marked disconnect between the live and recorded sound. This was to bring home to them the relationship between their gigs, their albums and audience expectation. Beer and Knightley determined from then on to achieve a balance between the musical realisation of their creativity and the practical constraints of touring: in effect to remain true to their roots as a duo.

For Beer and Knightley "the important thing is people don't go away thinking 'I loved it all stripped back and now it's got all this stuff on, or I loved it with all the stuff and I went to see them and it's all stripped bare!'" So whilst the stab at creating a radio friendly sound did not translate into airplay, nonetheless Beat About the Bush had a career defining impact on the pair. The insight they gained informed their understanding of how Show of Hands could both shape and meet audience demands as their career progressed.

Opposite: Appearances including Cambridge Folk Festival (1993)
Below: An early Show of Hands press shot taken in Corscombe, Dorset 1987 Manager, Gerard O'Farrell
PHIL: *"He's a very smart guy, he had an Australian degree in law, he could build a house and he's a very good musician himself, and he could also strip down a car and rebuild it."*

They would avoid the dilemma of "musicians who produce a rock level production sound who tour it to ninety people in a folk club or an arts centre feeling it's such a shame they can't do what they really want to do, which is make the sound of a greater number of musicians which an audience of five hundred and a fee of ten thousand would make possible." For Show of Hands learnt early that "Musicians have to come to terms with the number of people out there, the level of production they can afford to take on the road and what they really want to do in their heart."

The game-changing nature of this first 'concept tour' wasn't just confined to understanding those tensions between creativity and recording - then playing live and audience expectation - but through an audacious and radical plan outlined by a maverick Australian soundman. A trained opera singer and latterly post-punk popster, Gerard O'Farrell had recently moved into a ramshackle cottage on the edge of the Forest of Dean, becoming Beer's neighbour in the process. He stepped in to help out just over half way through the tour.

Formerly responsible for the in-house sound at Ronnie Scotts, O'Farrell had also worked with bands such as The Barely Works and The Poozies. After a few gigs with Beer and Knightley it was clear that there were inherent difficulties in the business set up. "We'd been in a situation where an agent had secured us a fat fee of £350.00 from a little theatre but the audience was only thirty people. Who gets to win there? The gig loses money on us – they're not going to book us again. It's not career nourishing on any level. We didn't get to go back to that theatre for five years." Then one night after a gig in Southport a well-known agent brazenly deducted an outrageous expenses claim from their fee - on top of his guarantee. Driving away O'Farrell said "If you want me to keep dealing with people like that - I'm out."

STEVE: *"Phil has always acted on certain principles, he's always believed that you should be self-contained in terms of your production. He never wants to rely on a sound engineer or a PA that has just been strung together. I think he's done so many thousand gigs where it was just nothing but grief. So he said that we'll always carry our own PA, even if we're playing in a pub. And the other thing he'd learnt from Ashley Hutchings in the 'Albion' band is to harvest people's names, always to run a mailing list. So on that principle you collect a lot of names and you're out there and being a self-contained entity, in other words you're quite easy to book.."*

PHIL: *"Knightley and I went out on this enormous rambling club tour, we were out for about 70 dates, and Steve was still teaching part-time so we were having to get back to Dorset so that he could go to school and teach, which was pretty knackering for him. Ralph came to see us two or three times and he rejected us to start with, and then finally said 'Actually yes, this would work really well'. So we ended up on a huge Ralph McTell tour...*

...Ralph's audience really was our target audience as well, and it got us playing in a very large number of quite beautiful theatres...We met quite a lot of people on this tour. What we discovered was that there are certain people who are not involved in the music business but will act in certain areas as promoters simply for their favourite acts. So we discovered in this case a couple of life-long friends - like Steve Nunn in the Norwich area...

...It was quite an experience. I learned a valuable lesson about less is more on that: you're on someone else's gig, you're trying to impress that person's audience; don't outstay your welcome; do not overdo it, do not think 'ooh maybe I can squeeze another number in' Say what you meant to say, play what you mean to play, get off. It worked extremely well and of course that subsequently created a life-long friendship with Ralph."

Beer and Knightley saw that to carry on with music business standard practice would mean risking a vicious cycle of diminishing returns, with possible loss of their soundman, bookings and audience numbers. On top of this in a genre that's rooted in gigs in small communities, members of which become good friends to the band – this standard practice would always be a potential source of antagonism. "We might say 'Look it's sold out, what are we getting for this gig?' or 'Look there are only three people here. Thank God we're getting a thousand!' Everybody's relationships are contentious. It's difficult for people to turn to their wife or husband and say 'I've booked a band for a thousand pounds and they want a PA, a hotel - and a rider. Something they might've taken on as a music-loving amateur suddenly becomes a financial risk. It causes tension in personal relationships. Plus the band turn up without knowing if the PA is any good. Or worried about what they might get to eat."

O'Farrell's disgust at sharp business practice inspired a brainwave that would lob Ralph McTells earlier advice into a higher orbit. McTell's idea of 'self containment' related to tours and albums connected through a single concept. O'Farrell's idea of 'self containment' related to a 'do-it-yourself' business model that is now held up as an aspirational ideal to musicians across the globe.

Above: Since his days running his own bands, Steve was used to organising his own accounts (however arcane...)

Left: Steve during a performance in the Theatre of the Hearts' 'The Oak', Beaminster, Dorset 1991

Opposite, top to bottom: Early gig, Soundman Will Thomas - part of the touring family, rides a motorbike on a tour of Australia, Ralph McTell, a crucial mentor for Show of Hands The whole crew line up with superfans Claire Rudd, Nick Pilley, Terri Anderson and Steve Sheldon, to celebrate attending their 100th Show of Hands gig. Their tour jackets were made by Terri to accompany their hand-made 'Show of Anoraks' Tshirts, which commemorated their first 50 gigs

Doing the opposite of beating about the bush, O'Farrell got straight to the point. "Look, I've been searching for a project to manage and you guys are it! But this is how we're going to work it. You're never going to charge a fee again. From now on we will attempt to regulate ticket prices and we will take 80 per cent of the net. We will turn up with our own PA, and soundman (me). We'll bring our own lights. Hell, we'll even bring our own rider. Obviously if no-one comes we lose money. But what this will do is empower a whole bunch of people to take a risk putting on a gig where they wouldn't before. And we lose the anxiety about bad technical quality affecting the performance." Beer and Knightley knew he was right. "Crucially from then on we stopped working for a fee. We worked for a percentage of the door. Still do. We take the risk. And so we get more gigs. In North Cadbury Village Hall they'll say 'What do you charge?' We say 'We don't charge. We just need a room for a hundred people and for you to take the ticket money.' People are empowered to put on shows – and a lot of people we empowered twenty years ago are now booking acts for their local theatres." (In 2014 Knightley began a two hundred date tour of village halls called 'Grow Your Own Gig' - still perfectly adopting this business model.)

PHIL: *"Gerard came up with a whole series of ideas, some of which were superb, some of which we thought were extremely 'far-out' at the time, but we liked his style and we thought this is the perfect situation, everything stays in-house. There's a one-stop place to go for everything to do with 'Show of Hands' and it's this guy. And it was brilliant."*

...I had seen every mistake in the book made in all the previous things that I'd ever been involved in, and I didn't want to repeat the same old same old. So pretty much from the start we decided that we would have this monolithic single management structure... I insisted that never again would we go anywhere without our own PA and we would be totally self-contained. We will no longer rely on anyone to do sound badly for us or any of those things, we will control those things. And sure enough we did that."

PHIL: *"There are still some of the things, quite clever things, that Gerard came up with that to this day we still use in our way of doing things. He said 'Right, you're no longer going to ask for fees, we're always going to work for percentages'. His argument was that it will empower more people to put on a gig when they know they're not guaranteeing you this money. It's also risky because if the gig falls flat on its face you're stuffed, but it also gives us then the leverage to drive up ticket prices. We thought, 'OK, we've got nothing to lose, so let's do that'. and he was right.."*

Opposite, left: Gerard's commitment to Show of Hands live sound would turn them into festival favourites
Opposite main: Phil, Gerard and Steve sampling their own self-provided backstage rider
Below: Media coverage grew along with the fanbase

NEWS, REVIEWS AND INFORMATION FROM THE WORLD OF TRADITIONAL MUSIC

ISSUE 24 • NOVEMBER • DECEMBER • 1997

THE LIVING TRADITION

UK £2.50 • USA $5 • CANADA $7

WIN CDs!

SHOW OF HANDS

IN THIS ISSUE
Folk Music on the BBC
Taffy Thomas
Phil & June Colclough
Gina LeFaux
Bluffers Guide to Sean-Nos

"We evolved a business structure that was part planning and part responding to what was in front of us. Now over time we've formalised it and become known as a 'cottage industry'." The self-reliance extended not just to live performance but also to recording and releasing albums. With O'Farrell, Beer and Knightley set up Hands On Music in 1996 that would release Show of Hands prolific musical output – taking care of both records and publishing.

Aware of the fundamental importance of an artistic aesthetic in the development of their career Show of Hands were delighted when a long time friend, the designer Rob O'Connor, founder of design company Stylorouge (whom Knightley had met when the two were students in Coventry), took on the design of the band's artwork, the flyers, the posters and the album covers. Their iconic look and feel quickly became as integral to the public perception of Show of Hands as the music.

As Beer, Knightley and O'Farrell set off on their journey without maps, they found that though in principle their plan was perfect, it would take about two years to really start working for them. Although their 1995 release Lie Of The Land (recorded by O'Farrell by the simple expediency of plugging the instruments straight into the desk and grabbing the live sound) received a 4 star "startlingly good" accolade from Q magazine and caused The Telegraph to mention their "formidable partnership", the three realised that their image worked against them. "Let's face it. We're not cool. If someone outlined Show of Hands to us as the evening's entertainment, I'm not sure we'd show up." Even O'Farrell, now enthusiastically installed as manager, assured them that "The idea of you two just doesn't appeal to anybody" and pushed home the point that he'd never have bothered to see them if he hadn't been asked to work for them first.

Left: 'Lie of the Land' album artwork and publicity photos
Top: Steve busy promoting the album
Above: On the set of the photoshoot with bird-handler (doubling as make-up artist!) Jonathon Marshall and model John Carpenter with Tess, the Harris Hawk

1994

✤ Beat About The Bush recorded – for the first time Show of Hands bring a 'band' on board, to fill out the sound. Produced by Mike Trim of Isis Records

✤ Gerard O'Farrell has moved to the UK, from Australia, where he had been pursuing his own music career. He is impressed by SOH and offers his services as their sound engineer before then becoming agent, manager and even record producer.

✤ Solid season of festival appearances

✤ Two-part tour promoting Beat About The Bush album

✤ Jay Turner and Malcolm Brittan were among the support artists on this tour

✤ A compilation of all the best material from the first three cassette releases are repackaged on one CD – Backlog 1987-1991

✤ Phil Beer also releases his first solo album, Hard Hats which gets a favourable review from Q magazine

✤ December show on home turf to end the year – Ralph McTell is the surprise guest at the Bridport concert

✤ Steve's songs are becoming popular with other artists – notably, The Albion Band, and Davey Arthur, who records versions of The Galway Farmer and Sit You Down

PHIL: *"We may have been the first, I don't know for sure, certainly one of the earliest bands and possibly the first within our genre, to have ever run an internet mailing list. It's entirely possible. Gerard embraced that from the absolute start."*

Above: Logo and homepage of Show of Hands 'Longdogs' fansite
Right: Steve and Gerard taking advice from friend Richard Patterson about the internet, digital marketing and building a Show of Hands website
Below: Customised merchandise honesty box

Bands building a career rely on media hype and the media, being unable to really write about the mechanics of music, write about lyrics and lifestyle, about the drugs, the domestic set ups and the band dynamics. There wasn't much copy in a couple of blokes in their early forties seemingly starting out as a band. Besides, Beer and Knightley preferred to keep their private lives private, though neither felt there was any mileage in mining them for glamorous tit-bits to attract the press. They knew they'd have to build their reputation another way.

And yet lifestyle is integral to the way Show of Hands steadily built their profile to win the Best Live Act at the BBC Radio 2 Folk Awards in 2004, the only award voted for by the public. (After which the public vote idea was dropped on the rumoured grounds that thanks to the dedication of their fans - they'd win every year). For in doing away with antagonistic relationships with their new model business plan, Show of Hands freed themselves and those they work with to enjoy the process and simply "have nice days." Plus, by enabling people to book them wherever they were from, whether the Nettlebed Folk Club, your local village hall or a concert hall, they removed barriers between them and their audience. Beer and Knightley were finding that through tireless gigging and founding their relationship with their audience on trust that its numbers were growing.

They demonstrated this trust from the outset by their method of selling cassettes at gigs. "We'd have a tub full of copies of our latest recording at the front of the stage, and announce: 'Help yourselves. Just bung in a fiver.'" And discovering demand often outstripped supply Show of Hands would turn up at gigs in their early days with a rack of Tascam tape copying machines and a paper-cutting guillotine. During a tour supporting Ashley Hutching's Albion Band, Knightley recalls rushing backstage to run-off extra cassettes and cut copies of the artwork to size whilst Beer was on stage for the main act.

Having learnt from Hutchings who asked people to leave their addresses if they'd like to be kept up to date with band news and upcoming gigs, Show of Hands slowly built up a database of fans who would receive a quarterly newsletter. Pre-internet it was all hands to the pump and unashamedly "roping-in friends' kids and local scallies to stuff envelopes and lick stamps," Knightley couldn't complain when one evening one of them ran off with his bike.

It was thanks to their fans and keeping them posted that in the spring of 1996 the Show of Hands gig at the Royal Albert Hall sold out – defying the gloomy predictions of the media pundits and the RAH staff, who, particularly bemused by the plan to stop the show and hold a raffle, thought Beer, Knightley and O'Farrell were mad.

Steve Sheldon's raffle in particular was a huge success. Its first-prize of a David Oddy hand-made instrument tied in with Show of Hands workshop tours, which the pair had started the previous year and in which Knightley and Beer shared their experience with fans and fellow musicians alike, deepening their connection with their audience. This connection was (and is) further enhanced by the intimacy of the annual Abbotsbury Festival, which Show of Hands put on for the first time in 1998. Featuring themselves and sets by special guests, they welcome the audience to spend the day with them at what feels like a private garden party. This sense of inclusion is integral to Show of Hands as they provide a real, appealing sense of community with their music at its heart.

STEVE: *"David Oddy's a really extraordinary man, he's in his mid-80s now. We met him probably in about 1979. He was one of these guys who still takes things to bits and mends them. In the late '70s he made a guitar for Paul Downes, which was beautifully constructed. It wasn't a particularly nice instrument but it was a fine piece of craftsmanship. He goes to the top of his little garden in Whipton and from this little shed emerges with these world-class instruments. But what he's most noted for is his plain speaking and slightly irascible Exeter nature. He says:'Bloody Phil Beer's a waste of space!' And if I go round he'll say 'Bloody Steve Knightley's a waste of space, and f***ing Paul Downes, bloody tossers'. He's very plain speaking, he likes to swear a lot when there's no ladies around. To David these aren't works of art, they're artefacts, they're just tools of the trade. 'If it breaks f***ing mend it, simple as that, it's just a bit of wire and wood'. But they are astonishing. And I suppose maybe 150 people now have seen me and Phil play the cello mandolin and bought one on the strength of it. He's got a loft full of instruments. He said to me the other day he's getting a bit frail and a bit unsteady on his feet. He said 'I think I've got one more cello mandolin I've got to make for you'. I already own 17 instruments hand-made by David... He quite likes me I think, there's no way of knowing with David. He comes to lots of gigs and he came to the Great Hall. We played to about 1,000 to 1,200 people and I said "Did you enjoy it?". He said "To be honest no, I don't mind Phil's fiddling but your songs are a bit dull".*

Show of Hands commitment to sound quality stretched to the actual manufacture of the tools of their trade - local craftsman David Oddy discovered his ability to craft excellent instruments following his retirement as a senior engineer at the Post Office.
Top: David Oddy, pictured in 1981.
Left: In his workshop in 2000, and previously shot in the same place in 1981.

1995

❖ In February, Steve and Phil instigate their inaugural workshop tour, demonstrating a strong commitment to sharing their hard-earned experience with fans, amateur enthusiasts and fellow musicians alike which will continue throughout the following years

❖ During the Spring and Summer – More touring and festival appearances, including playing to an audience of 12,000 at Fairport's Cropredy on August 10th

❖ The single Columbus (Didn't Find America) is released, with the beautiful and rarely heard instrumental B side Scattering Tears

❖ Steve and Phil go in the studio to record their Lie Of The Land album.
The Telegraph gives a very positive review, describing Show of Hands as a "formidable partnership" and Q magazine gives it four stars – "startlingly good"

❖ The band's snail-mail newsletter continues to be published and distributed to a growing fanbase, but following a crash course in all things internet, manager Gerard O'Farrell also launches the band's first website.

FARNHAM FOLK DAY

Saturday 13th May 1995

events kick off at 11.30am

putting Spring in your steps with major concerts, dances and workshops featuring

DOLORES KEANE
DEMBO KONTE, KAUSU KUYATEH & MAWDO SUSO (Gambia/Senegal)
Noel Hill (Ireland)
Kate Brislin
Ian Lowthian
Pete Morton
Chris Flitt

£18 on the door
and record stalls

ST. GEORGE'S ARTS FESTIVAL 1995

BECKENHAM
to 21st May 1995
Festival Programme
Parish Church of Beckenham
£1.50

TOM ROBINSON
259 Earlsfield Road, London SW18 4DE
Tel:01-818-704-302 Fax:01-818-750-778

... be back at home from June 5th. He's ... release in late summer, which will ... and it's REALLY GOOD !

There is one other act I have worked with in the last 6 months whom I'd warmly recommend as candidates for a small club tour. They are a duo called SHOW OF HANDS - both superb musicians and songwriters in their thirties who are building their reputation completely independently from the UK music biz. They manage their own business, have an enormous mailing list and play blindingly good shows to packed houses around the whole of Britain - even though the London music elite has hardly heard of them. They play a wide variety of unusual ethnic instruments, yet rock harder than most metal bands with an enormous wide-screen panoramic mountain of sound. If you're able to offer them a trial gig, however small, I can guarantee they'll blow any audience completely away. If you're interested contact Steve Knightley (+44/392-876-302) 56a Countess Wear Road, Exeter EX2 6LR

As for me, I'm writing songs for my next album, which we hope to record by the end of the year and plan to release ... spring 1996. I'm playing the Edinburgh Arts festival August 17-28th to ... and ... on tour in the UK for the whole of October (but no London shows till at least ... I think the fax modem on your computer has a prob... UK phones: it hears the double-ring, thinks it's a ... engaged to...and hangs up. I ... grabbing the phone on the first ring

Hope all's well with you.

Tom

GOSPORT EASTER FOLK FESTIVAL 1995

GUEST PASS

NAME/GROUP ....

DATE OF PERFORMANCE ....

SIGNATURE ....

MONDAY

GOSPORT

WINSLOW PUBLIC HALL
ELMFIELDS GATE, WINSLOW
FRIDAY DOORS 7.00 PM
17 NOVEMBER 1995

SHOW OF HANDS

UNRESERVED 125

ADVANCE £5.00(£4.00)
DOOR £6.00(£5.00)

TO BE RETAINED

ISIS RECORDS AND SHOW OF HANDS INVITE YOU TO THE LAUNCH OF THEIR NEW ALBUM

LIE OF THE LAND

THE BALLROOM AT THE BULL
EAST STREET, BRIDPORT, DORSET
TUESDAY 19TH SEPTEMBER
6pm 8pm

FOLLOWED BY A PERFORMANCE OF MATERIAL FROM THE ALBUM

CONDITIONS OF SALE
1. Latecomers may not be admitted until a suitable break in the performance.
2. The management reserves the right to make any cast or programme changes as necessary.
3. The management reserves the right to refuse admission
4. The use of cameras or any form of recording is forbidden.

THE HAULTH
SHOW OF HANDS
Folk Night
Guest   Admit One
Thu 09 Feb 95
9:15 PM
ONCE PURCHASED TICKETS CANNOT BE EXCHANGED FOR MONEY REFUND

SHOW OF HANDS
STEVE KNIGHTLEY & PHIL BEER

CRAWLEY BOROUGH COUNCIL
Leisure SERVICES
FOR THE BEST IN
ARTS AND ENTERTAINMENT

FOOTLIGHTS
Village Hall, West Chiltington

Show of Hands found their fanbase expanding as they were increasingly booked at festivals. Gig fit from playing in rowdy pubs where there was never a right to silence they knew how to enthrall a festival crowd. At Cambridge in 2001 they outstripped every other act on the bill when it came to selling CDs. Yet rather than reiterating any copyright warning, Show of Hands would say "Please feel free to make copies of our albums and give them to your friends." And thanked them for doing so. "It's not piracy but generosity!" Covering all bases, O'Farrell, who'd taken a crash course on using the internet when this was in its infancy, bucked the trend against music sharing on-line. He positively encouraged it as he set about building an on-line community.

Above: Steve taking charge of his own signage at Abbotsbury

STEVE: *"You look back and think:' Well there was a principle there'. We've created a community, which I think we have more than anyone else I can think of. We're both slightly alienated guys from either side of the Exe river, that's where we started from, from that same lower middle-class, upper working-class background. It's a similar environment, with the common touch but able to socialise at all sorts of levels. So it was a very fortunate alliance. And in order for it to work there must be something that is coherent at the heart of it, because we're not taking each other down a journey where the other one says 'I don't want to be here.'"*

1996

✤ Phil releases his second solo album, The Works, and the band's acoustic workshop in Exeter is released as a video programme

✤ The first Steve Knightley Songbook is published.

✤ A fan club is formed by Sue Morley and friends

✤ Spring; The First Royal Albert Hall show. The concert is recorded and released as an album in the autumn

✤ In May Vaughan Pearce joins the team handling CD manufacture and running the mailorder business as Show of Hands set up their own independent music distribution initiative – from now on, their music will be sold directly to their fans and followers – the first step towards starting their own record label, Hands On Music.

✤ Show of Hands are invited to present a number of workshops and concerts in Jakarta, Indonesia. They also play shows in Spain,

✤ September, dates in the USA

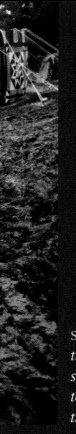

STEVE: *"At Glastonbury the PA and lights failed, and everyone just turned on their torches. People talk about that, a little tiny marquee gig we did, on the Avalon stage. The generators went so everyone just turned on their torches and we walked to the front of the stage, and people think that's like magic, we just carried on. So that was a moment...*

strings can break and then you have to change key, and you have to just own up and say gain'. There's been gigs where fights have broken out, Torquay Princess Theatre...
the way through. I was doing stories, setting up a song and he was going 'Yeah, yeah, yeah'. it was only about 8 rows back and I could hear him going ...... and I go 'This song is ...' Then with it' and the guy in front of him just smacked him in the mouth, dragged him into the aisle 'Hang on, whoa, house lights on please' and then it was 'It's not worth it Barry' and dragging t and it was all a bit tense because he had shouted out 'Just get on with it'. It was funny the hat doesn't happen very often. Do you know what we're going to do? We're going to go back 'Anyway, this song...' and a guy said 'Get on with it'! It was so quick that this guy recreated rilliant' and then we could carry on."

but we just know that you don't let the audience know. Every time you get on stage you e person has paid for that ticket and you just don't let your guard down. So hopefully no one s gone wrong. There are a few facial expressions that are passed between us all!"

1997

Say 'Yes' to Life
Say 'No' to Drugs

Ministry of Welfare, Govt. of India

five days in may

ENGLISH ACOUSTIC MUSIC

SHOW OF HANDS

Plus DAKOTA

(Concession)

RAISED

FRIORY PROMOTIONS presents
Five Days In May
SHOW OF HANDS
Chris Wood & Andy Cuttings, Kate Rusby
The Shepherds Bush Empire
Sunday 11th May 1997
Doors: 7:00pm
Tickets: £10.00
Row M   Seat 0023

Show of Hands Live
— also featuring —
JINKS' STACK
at the
PORT ISAAC POTTERY & GALLERY
SATURDAY 22nd NOVEMBER at 8.00pm
• All profits to the RNLI •

✤ February: The English Music Tour

✤ On February 6th filming starts for a full-length documentary about Show of Hands. Eventually to be called Stairway To Devon, the opening day is spent from dawn til dusk, following Steve and Phil, and their then merch manager Vaughan Pearce, travelling from the location of a gig in Hampshire to the Royal Pavilion in Brighton. The final shoot dates are 27-29th June, where Steve and Phil play at one of the muddiest Glastonbury Festivals ever.

✤ Five Days In May; a mini-tour showcases the talents of folk newcomers Kate Rusby and Chris Wood & Andy Cutting, along with SOH as the three acts rotate headline duties, with a flagship gig at London's Shepherds Bush Empire. It heralds the start of their ongoing commitment to bringing new talent on tour with them.

✤ In their spring newsletter, Show of Hands confirm in writing their support for 'home-taping', thereby bucking the music business's general policy of opposing such behaviour. The band always have considered the practice a pragmatic way to spread the word about their music, witnessing first hand that it boosts sales of tickets and CDs, underlining their truly independent music producer credentials.

✤ The Indian adventure – Steve and Phil embark on a short tour of hotels

✤ Another Cambridge Festival appearance for Steve and Phil…

✤ Dark Fields is released, along with the single Crazy Boy – a bold stab at securing national airplay

✤ Lighting tech Will Thomas joins the live crew – blazing a trail in live production for folk music

✤ Gigs in Spain

The band saw that spreading the word could translate into bums on seats and knew that receiving a copy of an album would inspire some people to get the real thing, not least for the covetable artwork. Show of Hands were finding that their business model worked from a village hall setting all the way up to a major venue – both here and abroad. For they were also discovering that their very locally rooted music (each track on 2003's The Path was linked to a specific West Country location) connected with audiences abroad as they gigged at clubs and festivals across Europe, Australia, America, India and the Far East.

Touring the Country Life album that featured Knightley's acclaimed anthemic title track in the Autumn of 2004, Miranda Sykes joined the duo, pinning down the harmonies with her melodic bass playing and lifting them with her beautiful crystalline vocals. She transformed Show of Hands, Beer and Knightley agree, "from a blokey duo into an indie folk band." Yet even as a trio they remained true to Show of Hands roots as a duo, with Sykes' contribution nourishing those roots so the music blossomed more fully. Country Life received the BBC Radio 2 Folk Awards nomination for best original song in 2005. And Sykes, on her way to becoming the duo's long time 3rd member, featured on Show of Hands follow up album, the best selling Witness.

Produced by Afro Celts' Simon Emmerson, Witness also garnered several award nominations, yet Show of Hands knew by now that whilst awards are gratifying in terms of recognition, when it comes to raising their profile and expanding their community it's still the gigs that matter most.

Above: Miranda (and cat) pictured during the Canada tour (2006)
Miranda before joining Show of Hands
PHIL: *"I still cannot remember the year she joined because I'm so used to having her around, it's been a long time"*
Opposite: The album sleeve for Witness and unused designs

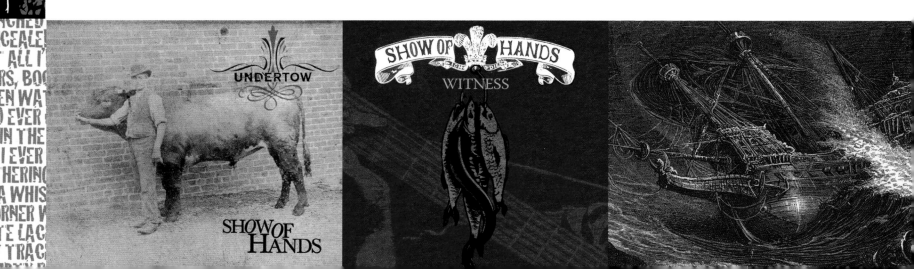

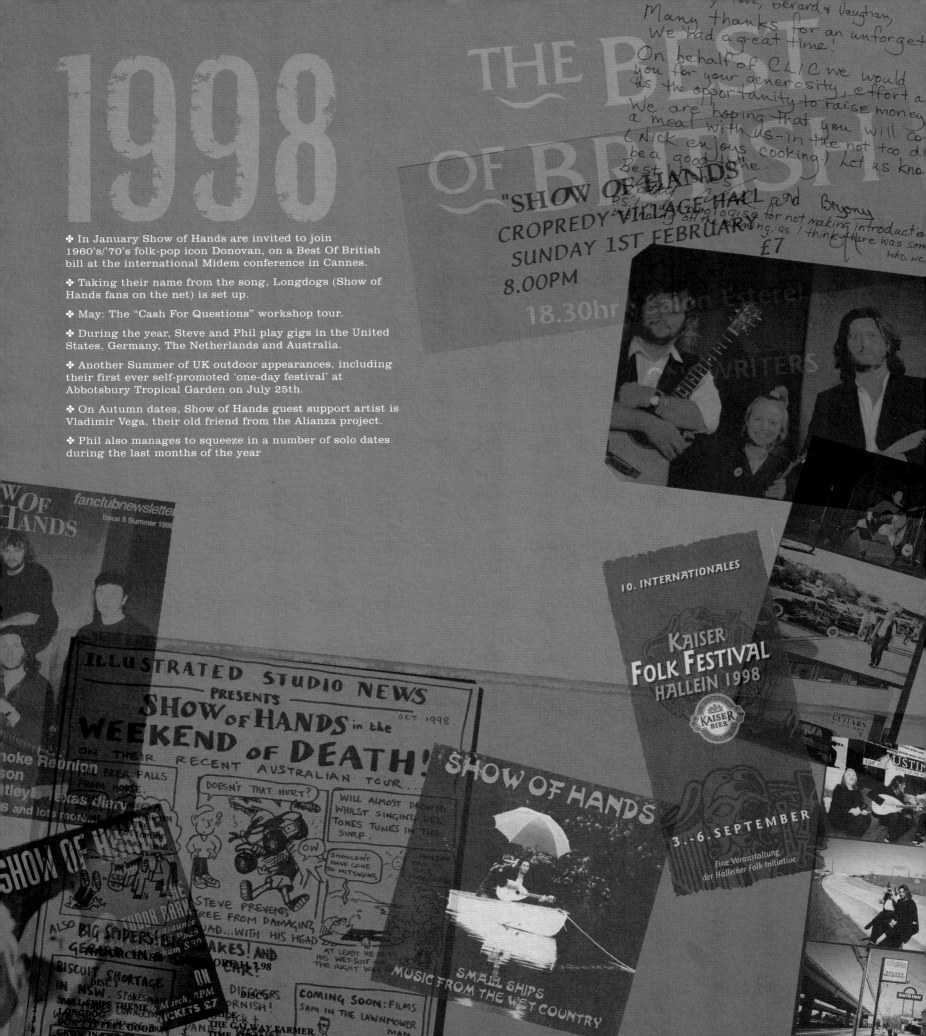

1998

❖ In January Show of Hands are invited to join 1960's/'70's folk-pop icon Donovan, on a Best Of British bill at the international Midem conference in Cannes.

❖ Taking their name from the song, Longdogs (Show of Hands fans on the net) is set up.

❖ May: The "Cash For Questions" workshop tour.

❖ During the year, Steve and Phil play gigs in the United States, Germany, The Netherlands and Australia.

❖ Another Summer of UK outdoor appearances, including their first ever self-promoted 'one-day festival' at Abbotsbury Tropical Garden on July 25th.

❖ On Autumn dates, Show of Hands guest support artist is Vladimir Vega, their old friend from the Alianza project.

❖ Phil also manages to squeeze in a number of solo dates during the last months of the year

STEVE: *"We are their soundtrack, and people come up all the time and talk about funerals and weddings and christenings. People come up and say 'So-and-so was ill for 18 months and all they played was your song, I Promise You'. Someone said that to me two nights ago; a guy with a life-threatening illness it was only 'I Promise You' - that the Winter won't last forever - that they kept playing. So you have to respect that and you have to internalise it and give it its due."*

Above: Show of Hands poster on display at Pontardewe Arts Centre for a gig in October 2006
Will Thomas and Vaughan Pearce at Abbotsbury 2002
Vaughan Pearce managed Show of Hands with his wife Gwen up until their retirement at the end of 2016
Left: Signing autographs in the Mojo tent at Cambridge (Matt Clifford in foreground)
Top left: Meeting fans and signing albums at St David's Hall, Cardiff in 2008

PHIL: *"At the point that Miranda came into it, when it was a well-established thing, that was because we had decided to put a big line-up together just for one festival season. We said from the outset 'We're going to do all these gigs as a 6-piece band, we told the world that's what we're going to do and it will end when it ends'. Miranda was the bass player and she stayed with it, because it was utterly logical and obvious from the way the thing sounds and the whole point of view that it gave us the one missing ingredient...*

...We first saw Miranda playing in a group called 'The Press Gang', who were very good. It was in Germany, on tour. She cropped up all over the place, she played with lots of people that I know, and I asked her to do just one or two of my occasional band gigs, so we already knew each other quite well. I called her up, she came over, we had an afternoon's rehearsal and that was it, that's all she needed, she was in, she did the rest of those dates. Then Steve suggested 'Do you think she might want to stick with it?' So she's been with us ever since."

MIRANDA: *" I first met Phil at Cropredy festival, I was hanging out beside the bar with my mum and Nick Quarmby was there. He said:'Phil is looking for a guitarist for the Phil Beer Band' you can play rhythm guitar... you only need three chords!" I said "Yeah, okay then," and Phil and I met up and played a bit and the rest is history really."*

"I was very young and during my time with the Phil Beer Band Pete Zorn was playing bass guitar in a Show of Hands band lineup when he had to leave. Phil said:'Well I know this bassist girl who has been playing in the Phil Beer Band.' I went and I did Wimborne Folk Festival and then Cambridge Folk Festival. Following the gig Steve said:'Oh, you've caused us a bit of a problem," and I was, like:'shit!, what have I done!?' I thought I had parked in the wrong place or something but he said:'well, you are really great, we like the mix of double bass and your backing vocals.'
So basically they kept me for the rest of the season. Then when they did the 2004 As you Were tour he invited me to be guest for that Autumn tour and then one or two of their Spring tour dates the following year, then I said:'look, you know, as long as I am not out of pocket and you give me £50 a night that covers my fuel then I would love to come and continue doing a few gigs with you' – and after that I became a proper member of the band."

1999

❖ The album Folk Music is released

❖ March: The Village Hall Tour

❖ The website continues to grow in popularity – free music downloads swell the number of visitors

❖ In August Steve and Phil play on The Cliff in Alderney during the eclipse

❖ Steve releases Track Of Words, his first solo album and goes on tour in support of the album

❖ Live dates overseas include venues in Australia and then Hong Kong and Kuala Lumpur Folk Festivals.

❖ Summer highlight is the Fylde Festival

Left: Miranda at Spalding Folk Club Singaround (circa 1997)

PHIL: *"There is a term that has cropped up over the years: "I don't like folk music but I like you guys", so you could jokingly say "We are folk music for people who don't like folk music"*

MIRANDA: *"...I was eight when I started to play. I lived rurally in Lincolnshire and in our primary school in one of our assemblies a group of peripatetic teachers came to our school and they were basically encouraging us little ones that we were entitled to 20 minutes of tuition a week on an instrument of our choice. I remembered this double bass in assembly. My mum and dad are musicians as well so she said: 'well, you could have lessons.' So I ended up being taken out of school by either my mum or my dad for 20 minutes of tuition a week in Spalding, seven miles from my little Primary School.*

"That carried on, me being classically trained, I didn't know what I wanted to do for a living. I went to the high school and then to sixth form. Mum noticed that things weren't really slotting in – I didn't know what I wanted to do so she said: 'there is this BTEC in Pop Music course'. So I went and studied that – but the course was a bit non-existent because the guy who ran it played in a Paul Weller tribute band so he was never around!"

THE ALBUMS

1987: **Show of Hands**

Beer and Knightley spent the Winter of '86/'87 in the recording studio above Knightley's garage at Catsley House recording songs for a cassette to sell at gigs. Simply entitled Show of Hands, this first album mostly featured Knightley's compositions, notably the much-lauded Exile with its sadly timeless resonance, rather than the covers that formed part of their live set.

From the get-go, Show of Hands demonstrate the beautiful depth and range of their musicality even as a duo, and their extraordinary ability to pen 'instant classics'. This is not, however, matched by their ability as graphic designers and on receiving a copy of the cassette, Rob O'Connor at Stylorouge (responsible for iconic album covers such as Blur's Parklife, Jake Bugg's On My One etc) offered to help out.

PHIL: *"We have two categories of albums, the main albums, and what we call the secondary albums, like 'Covers 1', 'Covers 2', which are not albums that we put out there or put any promotional work into, but nevertheless they're there for people to buy"*

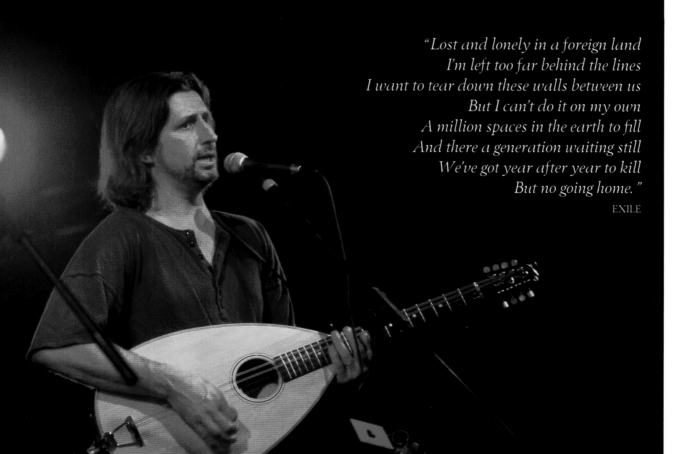

*"Lost and lonely in a foreign land
I'm left too far behind the lines
I want to tear down these walls between us
But I can't do it on my own
A million spaces in the earth to fill
And there a generation waiting still
We've got year after year to kill
But no going home."*

EXILE

2000

❖ Phil Beer Band tour
❖ Started recording at Mick Burch's Riverside Studio
❖ The first 'Covers' album is released

SHOW OF HANDS

in concert at the
MACREADY THEATRE
TEMPLE SPEECH ROOMS
RUGBY

(corner of Barby Road and Hillmorton Road)

Easter Monday, April 24th 2000

Admit One

ENGLISH FOLK
AND SONG SOCIETY
presents

SHOW OF HANDS

AT CECIL SHARP HOUSE
SUN 28TH MAY/2000
8.00PM
(DOORS 7.00PM)

000066

BARDENTREFFEN 25

Bavaria

SHOW OF HANDS

SATURDAY 15TH APRIL
Wreckers £7.00
7.45p.m.
WATERFRONT, ST. AUSTELL

EISTE IN GER ESTIVA

Folk on Tap

The Magazine of the
Southern Counties Folk Federation

SHOW OF
HANDS

ArtsLINK   Box Office
01276 707600

SHOW OF HANDS
THU 13-Jul-2000
AUDITORIUM

1990: **Tall Ships**

The launch of Tall Ships emphatically underlines Knightley's gift for an extended narrative. Using a West Country folk story to tell a tale of villagers wrecking ships for food in the aftermath of the Napoleonic Wars, Knightley brings history to vivid, pulsating life in the present. Written when he was a post-grad student in Brighton during the time he was gigging with Warwick Downes, it was a style of songwriting Knightley rejected in favour of '80s indie post-punk when he hit the London pub circuit. Asked to come up with a recording for a spot on Richard Digance's Capital Radio show, the presenter suggested Knightley perform Tall Ships and Knightley asked his friend and neighbour the actor Jim Carter (now known to the world as Downton Abbey's butler, Mr. Carson) to read the opening Wreckers' Prayer. Years later Beer and Knightley used the Capital Radio recording on this, their second outing on cassette, which featured traditional and self-composed songs on the 'B' side.

1991: **Out For The Count**

Having taken on Show of Hands, Bridport based agent Peter Wilson, suggested that the duo went to studios in Maisemore to self-produce an album that would enable the audience to essentially take the gig home. The songs were recorded in the order of the live set. "It was a case of 'if you liked that, here it is, here you go!' There was nothing between wanting and receiving." Peter Wilson may not have been aware of his resemblance to the actor Christopher Lee at the height of his Hammer Horror success but, as the album title suggests, any likeness was not lost on Beer and Knightley.

1992: **Show of Hands Live**

By the time Show of Hands came to record their first CD they had ramped up their performance into a stomping live set. The duo appeared at the popular live music night at the Bull Hotel in Bridport every Tuesday and had got to know local sound engineer Mike Trim. Trim recorded a gig at the venue in front of an invited audience and the result was released on The Road Goes On Forever label that he co-owned. A mix of traditional songs and Show of Hands originals, it features inspired contributions from Beer and Knightley's long time friends and collaborators including Matt Clifford and Paul Downes. The CD would be instrumental in securing Show of Hands a slot at Towersey Village Festival and many others that year where they romped home with the festival crowd. Drawing Ralph McTell down to see them play at Truro, the singer offered Show of Hands the coveted support slot to his upcoming 60-date tour. Sensing that their first CD would be their calling card to the next level of their career.

1992: **Alianza**

Produced by Beer and recorded at Ice House Studios in Yeovil, Alianza (The Road Goes On Forever) is the product of Beer, Knightley and Dave Townsend's (concertina) collaboration with three Chilean exiled musicians, Vladimir Vega, Sergio Avila and Mauricio Venegas. The project inspired Show of Hands classic song Santiago. Working with the Chileans opened Beer and Knightley to the exciting sonic possibilities of using non-traditional English instruments such as the cuatro and the horse's jaw, in their work as a duo – and importantly expanded their repertoire of rhythms. The Chilean street music with its hypnotic hip-swaying syncopated dance rhythms introduced a sensuous fluidity to the straight four-based rhythms Beer and Knightley typically worked with. Show of Hands would later describe themselves as 'World music from the West Country." It started here.

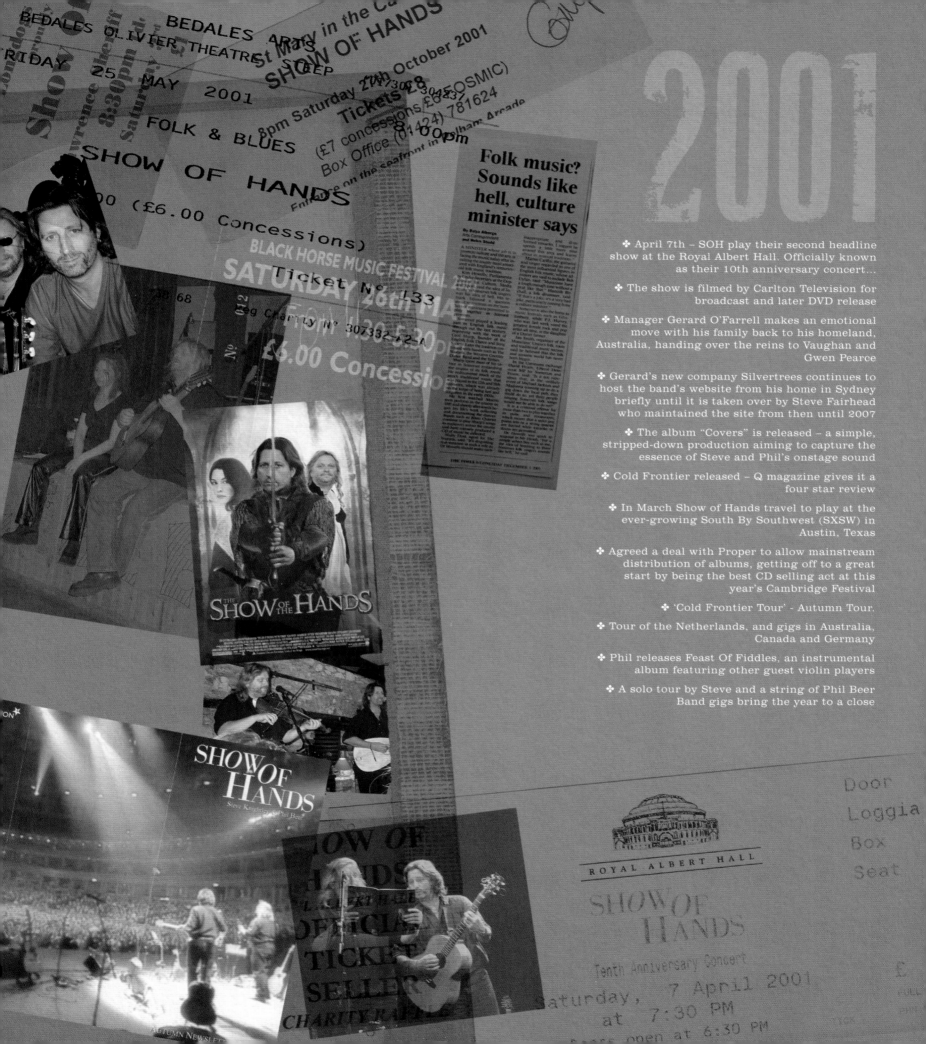

2001

BEDALES ARTS in the C...
BEDALES OLIVIER THEATRE
St Mary...
SHOW OF HANDS
...dep
FRIDAY 25 MAY 2001
8:30pm
8pm Saturday 20th October 2001
Tickets £8.00 (COSMIC)
(£7 concessions £6837
Box Office (01424) 781624
FOLK & BLUES
8.00pm

SHOW OF HANDS
£...00 (£6.00 Concessions)
Ticket Nº 133

BLACK HORSE MUSIC FESTIVAL 2001
SATURDAY 26th MAY
From 11.30 – 5.30pm
£6.00 Concessio...
Reg Charity Nº 307332-A2-A

Folk music? Sounds like hell, culture minister says

THE SHOW OF THE HANDS

SHOW OF HANDS
Steve Knightley Phil Beer

SHOW OF HANDS
OFFICIAL TICKET SELLER
CHARITY...

ROYAL ALBERT HALL
SHOW OF HANDS
Tenth Anniversary Concert
Saturday, 7 April 2001,
at 7:30 PM
Doors open at 6:30 PM

Door
Loggia
Box
Seat

❖ April 7th – SOH play their second headline show at the Royal Albert Hall. Officially known as their 10th anniversary concert…

❖ The show is filmed by Carlton Television for broadcast and later DVD release

❖ Manager Gerard O'Farrell makes an emotional move with his family back to his homeland, Australia, handing over the reins to Vaughan and Gwen Pearce

❖ Gerard's new company Silvertrees continues to host the band's website from his home in Sydney briefly until it is taken over by Steve Fairhead who maintained the site from then until 2007

❖ The album "Covers" is released – a simple, stripped-down production aiming to capture the essence of Steve and Phil's onstage sound

❖ Cold Frontier released – Q magazine gives it a four star review

❖ In March Show of Hands travel to play at the ever-growing South By Southwest (SXSW) in Austin, Texas

❖ Agreed a deal with Proper to allow mainstream distribution of albums, getting off to a great start by being the best CD selling act at this year's Cambridge Festival

❖ 'Cold Frontier Tour' - Autumn Tour.

❖ Tour of the Netherlands, and gigs in Australia, Canada and Germany

❖ Phil releases Feast Of Fiddles, an instrumental album featuring other guest violin players

❖ A solo tour by Steve and a string of Phil Beer Band gigs bring the year to a close

Top and left: Steve and Phil
recording tracks for the album 'Covers 2'
at the Suffolk home of friend,
software designer, Richard Patterson
Above: Phil with Simon Emmerson
co-producer of the Witness album at
Presshouse Studio, Colyton, Devon 2007

2002

✤ Steve tours with Martyn Joseph and Tom Robinson as
'Faith, Folk & Anarchy'

✤ Second volume of 'The Steve Knightley Songbook' is published

✤ Toured Scotland and the North East for the first time.

✤ SOH On The Level Tour

✤ Phil undertakes a short tour with Paul Downes,
his original musical partner and long-term SOH collaborator

✤ Recent live favourites, including My Brother Jake,
The Somme Trilogy and Crow On The Cradle are
included on a new album, Cold Cuts

✤ Phil Beer releases a live album "Mandorock Live" recorded on
his Phil Beer Band tour of 2000

✤ Summer schedule includes Trowbridge, Brampton,
Warwick, a rainy Sidmouth and the annual Show of Hands
knees-up at Abbotsbury

✤ They also guest at a Summer concert at the
Eden Project in Cornwall

✤ Tour of the Netherlands, and gigs in Australia,
Canada and Germany

✤ Phil gigs with both the Phil Beer Band and with Deb Sandland,
while Steve undertakes some dates with Martyn Joseph

✤ In August Steve and Clare get married

✤ Meanwhile... elsewhere in the UK,
Bass player Miranda Sykes is gigging with
folk-rock band Press Gang

SAT 17TH AUGUST 2002
SHOW OF HANDS
AT THE
eden project

PHIL ON STEVE (circa 1970): "Even at this
early stage I could see there was something
special about Knightley. It's the obvious thing:
that he was the one who was writing songs at
that stage and was heavily into Bob Dylan. We
sometimes make a joke about playing Steve's
first song, which contains every Bob-ism – leaving
on the morning train, etc – every possible cliché
that can possibly be contained in late '50s, early
'60s American style songwriting is absolutely
encapsulated in Knightley's first song and we
make a bit of a comedy event of this sometimes.
We have played it at gigs, yes, once or twice and
it is very funny. What you do is get the audience
to anticipate the rhyme in the word that's
coming next and they get it about 80% of the
time because it's so predictable. 'I'm leaving on
the morning train... babe', that one crops up – 'I
didn't wanna hurt you... babe'. Very funny"

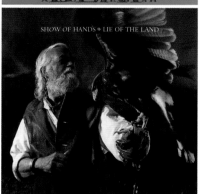

1994: **Beat About The Bush**

After their successful tour with Ralph McTell, Mike Trim proposed a new recording with a radio-friendly sound. "The thinking was you had to have a rhythm section and percussion to get airplay and on the whole, that's right." At Wytherstone Studios in West Dorset, Beer and Knightley were joined by Nick France on drums, and several musician friends including Vladimir Vega who augmented the line up. Setting the working practice for their subsequent career, they agreed: "If you employ a producer, you have to trust their vision," noting "Mike had a vision; he invested in it and in us." Featuring standout tracks The Galway Farmer and Armadas that shine with Knightley's keen eye for fact and historical truth, the record came out on Trim's own label Isis, to be re-released in 1999 on the bands own Hands On Music.

1995: **Lie Of The Land**

Now working with Gerard O'Farrell as soundman and manager, the duo went back into the studio, this time to Free For Good Studios near Tewkesbury, with O'Farrell also producing. "He said: 'Sod all the overdubs, I'm going to record you as you play live.'" It was slightly unnerving for Beer and Knightley as recording in a studio meant the chance to give rein to their perfectionism and polish the sound. But O'Farrell was having none of it. The theme of the album was Dorset songs. Knightley could clearly see the lie of the land in the place each track sprang from, he knew the exact fields The Hunter crossed, the shoreline where the preacher walked. He penned country tales, Hardyesque portraits of rural villains. The arresting artwork featured photos of Knightley's erstwhile teaching colleague – a keen falconer. "A bloke with a beard and a hawk!" And life also tipped a wink to art when during the mastering of The Preacher in Taunton, a hearse crashed through the studio window. Using the latest technology, the recordings had been made on DAT, but the pair thought a cassette copy of the album sounded better. So Beer took the DAT to RealWorld Studios and spent half a day running it through an analogue mastering machine to warm it up. That's the version that was released on Isis to acclaim from the music press. That acclaim could have helped with promotion: "A review said I had a vast and windswept voice. In advertising our gig, one venue just used 'vast and windswept' and a picture of us."

STEVE: *"I can look back now and see that there is a structure that I can now work to, but at the time you're not quite aware of it. You can take an everyday expression like 'Are we alright' and that's become quite a big song of ours. So there are these everyday expressions, and I've got another one at the moment called 'Make The Right Noises' or you can do a 'Galway Farmer', like a narrative song, or 'The Preacher' – let's take a Portland preacher who's in love with a miner's wife who prays for an accident and then it comes true. So you can work that through."*

1996: **Live At The Royal Albert Hall**

O'Farrell's recording "off the desk" of the band's audacious debut at the Royal Albert Hall outsold all Show of Hands previous albums. Like all their subsequent releases, Live At The Royal Albert Hall was put out on the band's own label Hands On Music, run by O'Farrell.

1997: **Dark Fields**

Again the songs sprang from the duo's connection with the West Country and Knightley's avid exploration of local history, expressing themes that resonate way beyond the specific time and place from which they spring. Big songs like Cousin Jack, Longdog and the eponymous title track featuring Chris While's beautiful duet with Knightley, all made their recording debut here. The Train, however, sprang from Show of Hands' tour of India earlier that year and a journey on which they met a man travelling to Hyderabad who, separated from his family during the chaos and bloodshed of partition, was travelling to see them for the first time in fifty years. Recorded in Joe Partridge's Cornwall studio, the album featured contributions from old friends like Matt Clifford and new ones including Kate Rusby, Chris Wood and Andy Cutting all of whom Show of Hands were to help in establishing their careers. Crazy Boy was released as the band's first single without troubling the charts. Selling the CDs at gigs, the band gave away blank cassettes saying "tape them, by all means, spread the word!" until an injunction from Universal came winging their way: track 10 was Farewell Angelina. "They said you can give away your own music but you can't give away Bob Dylan's!" David Juniper provided the iconic 'Wicker Man' illustration.

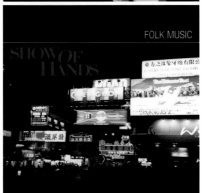

PHIL: "'Covers 1' actually wasn't live, we didn't even use multi-track, we moved into a village hall with some basic recording gear and recorded two days of straightforward performances, played live, straight to stereo. I have boxes and boxes of performance stuff still to be gone through. One day we'll have to dust off the dat machine and actually start playing some of them and see what happens. There's an awful lot of material that I guess it would be really difficult ever to revisit again which is rather a shame."

1998: Folk Music

Like it says on the tin, this album is a recording of folk songs performed just by the duo in a celebration of the music that inspired them as teenagers doing the rounds of the local folk circuit. Plus a pared-down re-working of The Train/Blackwater in traditional English style.

2000: Covers

Marking the millennium with a celebration of music that inspires them, in Covers Beer and Knightley give beautiful acoustic renditions of songs from artists as diverse as Tom Robinson, Peter Gabriel, Thom Yorke and Ray Davies to Bob Dylan, Billy Joel and Lowell George. Whilst testifying to eclectic influences from beyond the folk genre, these tracks shine with their nuanced, folk-inspired approach. Recorded live by O'Farrell in Chudleigh Town Hall, the sound has a direct warmth and immediacy.

2001: Cold Frontier

As the increasing productivity of Hands On Music demanded more of O'Farrell's time, Beer and Knightley's old friend Mick Dolan (whom Beer had met when Dolan was working as Steve Winwood's house engineer) took care of the sound on the live dates. Dolan also owned some excellent portable recording equipment and set it up at Show of Hands mate Mick Burch's split-level house on the banks of the Exe with fantastic views across the river. It was an apt setting to record The Flood, with its themes of flooding intertwined with the perils of migration and the need to find our common humanity as people search for work. Cold Frontier, the title track of the album, again highlights Knightley's deft hand with historical narratives that resonate with current meaning.

This time the reviews noted that the polished production, though pared back (and featuring just three guest musicians including John Redmond on bodhran) smoothly integrated world instruments into English and Gaelic rooted songs. World music from the West Country was becoming a 'thing'.

2002: Cold Cuts

Touring Cold Frontier, Mick Dolan recorded their live performances that featured new arrangements of the duo's 'old' songs and other of their gems that had fallen by the wayside. Applying their fresh approach to covers such as Leonard Cohen's, "First They Take Manhattan" that were also to appear on Cold Cuts, the album was released to critical acclaim in July 2002.

*"In the faces under the skin
Of all those who've worked this land
You'll find the traces of all who've been
They lie so close to hand
Let the borders fall after all these years
to my cold frontier..."*
COLD FRONTIER

2003: **The Path**

The South West Path winds along the coast from Minehead all the way around Cornwall and up to Poole in Dorset. Historically trod by the coastguard on the look out for smugglers, it opened as a designated trail in 1978. This album of instrumental songs, named for places along the route, allowed Knightley and Beer to mine their combined love of the sea and the West Country for musical inspiration.

2003: **Country Life**

Earning Knightley the moniker "the gravel voiced spokesman of the rural poor" Country Life was inspired by an experience he'd had renovating his thatched cottage in Whitchurch Canonicorum. Pat Symes, a local craftsman who'd pitched up to help, told him "I was born here" assuming (incorrectly) that Knightley was doing-up a holiday home. The plight of new generations of local people priced out of their own homes and the tough realities of rural life inspired this breakthrough album. It was recorded again at Mike Burch's Riverside Studio on and off over six weeks, with Mick Dolan also at the helm using the best recording technology to turn in a glittering Jackson Browne-influenced production. Country Life again seamlessly mixed Latin, Celtic and blues nuances with elements of English traditional music in their compelling 'world music from the West Country' sonic landscape. It landed them a slot on BBC Five Live special with Matt Bannister and gained them a fan in Andrew Marr, (though he has yet to vacate his holiday home).

STEVE: *"Country Life' changed a lot of things, because then we became known as an 'issues' band and I became known as an 'issues' writer, and we were on Farming Today and Tom Heap and anything to do with agriculture or the rural economy. Andrew Marr wrote about 'Country Life'. We were getting known but not necessarily getting radio play."*

Steve, Phil and producer Mick Dolan at
Mick Burch's Riverside Studio during the
recording of 'Country Life'

Right: 'Country Life' album cover image (Steve's wife Clare and son Jack appear outside the caravan)
Below: Behind the scenes at the 'Country Life' shoot with Director Rob O'Connor and Producer Tod Grimwade

ROB O'CONNOR on Country Life: *"When Steve played me the first songs for Country Life I was completely transported to his world – themes so rooted in his rural environment, and words as tender as they are raw and visceral. In the design studio at Stylorouge we immediately embarked on our initial ironic pastiches of Country Life magazine, but this project felt like a much more important beast – it required imagery that cut deep into the issues that the songs tackled – the shameful exploitation and destruction of country communities in the name of consumerism and gentrification, the betrayal of the people both old and young whose blood, sweat, fraternity and laughter had built these communities and who now yearn to find love and compassion where only memories seem to provide a home for such things... at one point I suggested to Steve the alternative title 'Countrycide'...*

... I somehow persuaded the guys to buy into a major commitment – a combined photo and video shoot on location, using the real inhabitants of their own Devonshire localities to add a journalistic realism to Steve's painfully topical lyrics.

I took to the West Country and with my producer friend Lou's local knowledge and our photographer Bernd's hard hitting gritty style, we nailed the brief in a three day trip that culminated in a rousing performance shoot with Phil, Steve and friends in a disused barn outside Topsham. Cameraman Tod Grimwade and my fellow art director from Stylorouge Chris O'Hare completed the team in Devon, and designer Mark and video editor Jamie were waiting to get their hands on the results back in London. Although we were a small crew we had respectful, helpful talent and it felt like proper film-making...

During the dressing of the barn prior to the performance shots, Chris and I photographed the last couple of people for the inside of the album cover ourselves, as Bernd had already returned to London. And as luck would have it, a man turned up to deliver equipment for the shoot. Jumping down from the cab of his lorry he asked me where the stuff should go. He was dressed for work, bald headed, muscular and tattooed. His name was Karl, but to me, he was Terry from the song Red Diesel, serendipitously dropped into our little set from God-knows-where to become the cover star for the album. So ironically, none of our officially hired locals made it onto the front cover, and nor did Berndt take the final shot. Such is the nature of chance and the power of collaboration. Country Life provided me with an authentic, meaningful creative project; an album, a cover and a video that all remain among my personal favourites."

Right: Steve and Miranda, Norwegian Church, Cardiff Bay, 9th April 2006
Bottom: Steve at Presshouse Studio with Simon Emmerson during the recording of the 'Witness' album

2005: **As You Were**

Again Mick Dolan recorded performances on the band's Autumn tour which took place in November 2004 and featured stellar contributions from bassist Miranda Sykes.

2006: **Witness**

At the BBC Folk Awards one year, Beer and Knightley fell into conversation with AfroCelt Sound System co-founder Simon Emmerson, who was thinking about moving to Frome. Knightley persuaded him that Bridport was better and Emmerson duly turned up. Co-producing Witness with fellow AfroCelt Simon "Mass" Massey, they brought the AfroCelts huge sample library to play on Knightley's organic songs of local life that spoke to wider socio/political issues. As well as adding to the mix ambient sounds recorded in the studio – such as as a squeaky chair, Emmerson and Massey broadened Show of Hands musical sound-world with electronica and Senegalese, Caribbean and Latin American elements. With these they created a cinematic musical realisation of the narrative songs. Miranda Sykes cemented her place in the band, contributing to ten of the tracks including Roots and The Dive, and a host of outstanding guest musicians added to the overall brilliance of the sound. Introducing drums and percussion for the first time since Beat About The Bush, the sampled rhythms drove the timeless feel of the production. Whilst heavily populated and painstakingly arrived at, it yet feels free, spacious and effortlessly cool. Remaining rooted in place, Witness nonetheless crossed musical borders drawing a new audience and fresh critical acclaim to Show of Hands, becoming their best selling album to date.

2007: **Roots: The Best of Show of Hands**
A 'best of' double album celebrating 20 years since they set out on the road as Show of Hands, the first CD 'Short Stories' features favourite tracks from the band's releases to date (bar Out For The Count) with the second CD 'Longdogs' consisting of tracks chosen by their fans

2008: **Live at Exeter Phoenix**
Recorded on Saturday 8th. December 2007 the record was released on Show of Hands fans – Longdogs own label to raise money for the national childhood cancer charity CLIC Sargent and the paediatric oncology fund at Bramble Ward in the Royal Devon and Exeter Hospital. Learning of Knightley and his wife Clare's five year-old son Jack's diagnosis with acute lymphoblastic leukaemia, the fans immediately rallied to help. The release of the album was just one example of their many initiatives of practical support. (Jack was given the all clear in 2016).

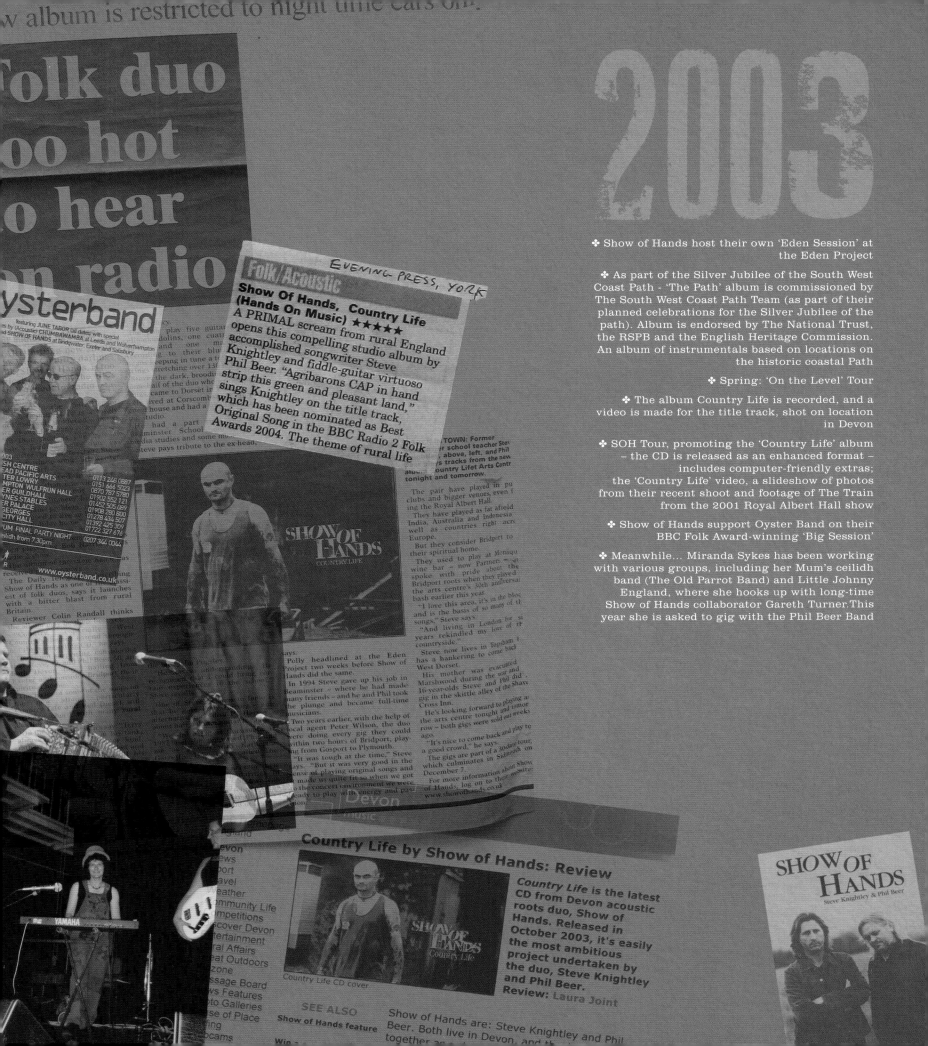

2003

w album is restricted to night time ears off.

Folk duo oo hot o hear on radio

Oysterband
featuring JUNE TABOR (all dates) with special
and SHOW OF HANDS at Bridgwater, Exeter and Salisbury
play five guitar
mandolins, one cuatro
and one ma
to their blu
keeping in tune a t
stretching over 130
the dark, broodi
lf of the duo who
came to Dorset in
ved at Corscomb
house and had a
studio.
had a part
minster School
dia studies and some mu
teve pays tribute to the ex-head,

03
SH CENTRE
AD PACIFIC ARTS 0113 248 0687
TER LOWRY 0151 666 5023
MPTON WULFRUN HALL 0870 787 5780
ER GUILDHALL 01902 552 121
YNES STABLES 01452 505 089
ER PALACE 0190B 280 800
GEORGES 01278 434 507
CITY HALL 01392 425 309
01722 327 678
UM FINAL PARTY NIGHT
lidh from 7.30pm 0207 344 0044

www.oysterband.co.uk

The Daily
Show of Hands as one of
est of folk duos, says it launches
with a bitter blast from rural
Britain.
Reviewer Colin Randall thinks

EVENING PRESS, YORK

Folk/Acoustic

Show Of Hands, Country Life (Hands On Music) ★★★★★

A PRIMAL scream from rural England
opens this compelling studio album by
accomplished songwriter Steve
Knightley and fiddle-guitar virtuoso
Phil Beer. "Agribarons CAP in hand
strip this green and pleasant land,"
sings Knightley on the title track,
which has been nominated as Best
Original Song in the BBC Radio 2 Folk
Awards 2004. The theme of rural life

TOWN: Former
r school teacher Stev
, above, left, and Phil
s tracks from the new
Country Lifet Arts Centr
tonight and tomorrow.

The pair have played in pu
clubs and bigger venues, even f
ing the Royal Albert Hall.
They have played as far afield
India, Australia and Indonesia
well as countries right acr
Europe.
But they consider Bridport to
their spiritual home.
They used to play at Moniqu
wine bar — now Partners — gt
spoke with pride about the
Bridport roots when they played
the arts centre's 30th anniversar
bash earlier this year.
"I love this area, it's in the bloc
and is the basis of so many of th
songs." Steve says.
"And living in London for si
years rekindled my love of th
countryside."
Steve now lives in Topsham
has a hankering to come bac
West Dorset.
His mother was evacuated
Marshwood during the war and
16-year-olds Steve and Phil did
gig in the skittle alley of the Shave
Cross Inn.
He's looking forward to playing a
the arts centre tonight and tomor
row — both gigs were sold out weeks
ago.
"It's nice to come back and play to
a good crowd," he says.
The gigs are part of a 30date tour,
which culminates in Sidmouth on
December 7.
For more information about Show
of Hands, log on to their website
www.showofhands.co.uk

Polly headlined at the Eden
Project two weeks before Show of
Hands did the same.
In 1994 Steve gave up his job in
Beaminster — where he had made
many friends — and he and Phil took
the plunge and became full-time
musicians.
Two years earlier, with the help of
local agent Peter Wilson, the duo
were doing every gig they could
within two hours of Bridport, play
g from Gosport to Plymouth.
"It was tough at the time," Steve
says. "But it was very good in the
ense at playing original songs and
made us quite fit so when we got
the concert environment we were
eady to play with energy and pas

Devon
Music

Country Life by Show of Hands: Review

Country Life is the latest
CD from Devon acoustic
roots duo, Show of
Hands. Released in
October 2003, it's easily
the most ambitious
project undertaken by
the duo, Steve Knightley
and Phil Beer.
Review: Laura Joint

Country Life CD cover.

evon
ws
port
avel
eather
ommunity Life
mpetitions
scover Devon
tertainment
at Affairs
eat Outdoors
zone
ssage Board
ws Features
to Galleries
se of Place
ing
bcams

SEE ALSO
Show of Hands feature

Show of Hands are: Steve Knightley and Phil
Beer. Both live in Devon, and th
together 30

Win

❖ Show of Hands host their own 'Eden Session' at the Eden Project

❖ As part of the Silver Jubilee of the South West Coast Path - 'The Path' album is commissioned by The South West Coast Path Team (as part of their planned celebrations for the Silver Jubilee of the path). Album is endorsed by The National Trust, the RSPB and the English Heritage Commission. An album of instrumentals based on locations on the historic coastal Path

❖ Spring: 'On the Level' Tour

❖ The album Country Life is recorded, and a video is made for the title track, shot on location in Devon

❖ SOH Tour, promoting the 'Country Life' album – the CD is released as an enhanced format – includes computer-friendly extras; the 'Country Life' video, a slideshow of photos from their recent shoot and footage of The Train from the 2001 Royal Albert Hall show

❖ Show of Hands support Oyster Band on their BBC Folk Award-winning 'Big Session'

❖ Meanwhile... Miranda Sykes has been working with various groups, including her Mum's ceilidh band (The Old Parrot Band) and Little Johnny England, where she hooks up with long-time Show of Hands collaborator Gareth Turner. This year she is asked to gig with the Phil Beer Band

SHOW OF HANDS
Steve Knightley & Phil Beer

2009: Arrogance Ignorance And Greed

Enjoying the unexpected elements that a producer could bring to the table, Show of Hands brought in Stuart Hanna of Megson, for their next studio album on the recommendation of Seth Lakeman. Although Witness with its AfroCelt pedigree seemed like a departure from their usual sound, compared to AIG it sits more happily with their body of work. Stuart Hanna recorded Knightley singing Rain Go Away when Knightley had just got up and had a sore throat. Hanna said: "OK great, that's it." "What do you mean, I've just got up and I've got a sore throat!" "Yep, great, that's the sound I want. I know what you're like. I know how you're perceived. Everything slick and beautifully produced. I want it to sound ugly." His raw post-punk aesthetic suited the often polemical and angry tone of the songs, in which Knightley shows the simple human element behind tsunamis of social consequence. The title track encapsulates the seed of the global market crash with the line "All I wanted was a home"– highlighting the basic human need fuelling the sub-prime crisis that exposed the bankers greed. Whilst sharing the public outrage springing from issues that inspire him, Knightley doesn't channel that anger as he writes: "It's a craft," he says: "When writing songs you have to be dispassionate to make them work." And with the clarity that approach offers, his songs themselves become a channel for public anger, like opening a valve on a pressure cooker. They articulate feeling and focus response to a social issue. In AIG Knightley deftly pulls together his natural inclination to share knowledge with the strands of his songwriting ambition – to inform and educate through entertainment. He appreciated the way Hanna approached the songs as a director might a play – "OK, sing it like you've just written it and aren't quite sure if it works..." – for this played to Knightley's awareness of the benefit of fresh perspectives. Beer found his perspective changed too. Hanna's extraordinary ability as a string arranger and fine harmonic sensibility indelibly altered Beers approach to his own multi-string work.

The up-front edginess of AIG that garnered awards and critical acclaim gave mainstream media viewers a taste of how world music from the West Country can jump the barriers. Watching the Andrew Marr show or listening to national radio, they realised it might have an accent, but it speaks for them too.

✤ Phil starts the year with a Phil Beer Band tour

✤ Show of Hands are Winners of 'Best Live Act' at BBC2 Folk Awards – the result of a public vote

✤ Country Life album released

✤ An augmented line-up is put together for the Summer festivals. Guest musicians are Pete Zorn (electric bass, sax & percussion), Matt Clifford (keyboards) and Rom Dobbs (drums). After a last-minute call up from Richard Thompson, Pete leaves to be replaced by Miranda Sykes (double bass, electric bass & vocals).

✤ 'Country Life' Up Close Tour – smaller more intimate venues

✤ July – The line-up for Abbotsbury includes Seth Lakeman, Kerfuffle, Chris While & Julie Matthews and compere Keith Donnelly

✤ Festivals include Trowbridge, Warwick, Cambridge and Cropredy

✤ TV coverage of the band from the Cambridge Festival courtesy of the Beeb

✤ Aug 27th – another 'Eden Project' appearance, this time as part of the Womad Session

✤ Autumn Tour – Miranda Sykes appears as a special guest

✤ Steve tours with Seth Lakeman and Jenna in support of their collaborative album "Western Approaches"

✤ Phil releases a solo album; Rhythm Methodist and tours with Deb Sandland and the Phil Beer Big Band

✤ Show of Hands "On Film" DVD comprises the Big Gig (2001 Royal Albert Hall show), the Stairway To Devon documentary, and various promo videos

✤ Steve plays dates with Martyn Joseph, the tour culminating in a one-off reunion with Tom Robinson completing the Faith, Folk and Anarchy line-up

✤ Steve and Phil throw a joint 50th Birthday Party at The Globe Hotel in Topsham

Andrew Marr
Notebook

☐ IT'S A sign of being older and more pathetic, but this was the summer when I finally discovered the wet suit.

Sea-bathing off the pebbly beaches of south Devon is a perpetual delight, but it had never struck me before that it isn't absolutely necessary to go through the gasping pain of icy waves. A wet suit isn't ... and, given the weather this August, you didn't even need to take it off afterwards.

In many ways, the Devon coast seems to be getting more prosperous. House prices are crazy; bistros and chi-chi food shops abound; in converted mills and expanding "farm markets", one can buy local red wine, exotic cheeses, excellent meat and bread so handwoven and resilient it could be used to build cottages. It has always been a naturally rich part of the world: back in the 1660s, Thomas Fuller was lauding its plentiful and "most toothsome" strawberries, which he recommended with claret wine or "sweet cream".

The other side of the modern story is less obvious – collapsing farm incomes and local families priced out of small towns and villages. We bought a CD by a Devon folk band, Show of Hands, which made us wince as we drove home: *"The red brick cottage where I was born/ Is the empty shell of a holiday home/ Most of the year there's no one there/ The village is dead and they don't care.../ If you want cheap food well here's the deal/ Family farms are brought to heel".* It was a tart reminder that there's more to the politics of the countryside than foxhunting.

CROPREDY MUSIC FESTIVAL™ 2

THURSDAY 12th AUGUST
6.30pm - 11.00pm

OYSTERBAND
JACKIE LEVEN & MICHAEL COSGROVE
MOSTLY AUTUMN · BLUE MEANIES

FRIDAY 13th AUGUST
12 noon - 12 midnight

JETHRO TULL
SHOW of HANDS
THE JERRY DONAHUE BAND
AnnA ryder & STEVE TILSTON BAND
WITH MARTIN ALLCOCK & CLIVE BUNKER
THE FAMILY MAHONE · EARL OKIN
ANDY GUTTRIDGE BAND

SATURDAY 14th A
12 noon - 10 midnight

Fairport Conven
∞ SPECIAL
RICHARD DIGAN
NICK HARPER
THE MORRIS ON BAN
FEATURING ASHLEY HUTCH
JEZ LOWE & THE BAD PENN
THEMIGHTYFIREBIRDS
GO LADY

TICKETS:

Steve Knightley (left) and Phil Beer

Controversial so... local duo

A controversial new s... will be heard in ... Ilfracombe on November 25th in the wake of the U.S. elections - when Devon's own award-winning acoustic duo Show of Hands return to the Landmark Theatre...

THE TOAST

(with little factual accuracy and with apologies to Stanley Holloway, John Betjeman… well, everyone really…)

If we ever chance to motor west
We chuck our berets, boots and vests
and drive to sunny Devonshire,
On this occasion, Topsham here,
To see our friends of 30 years,
Mr. Knightley, Mr. Beer.

For Phil, this bustling urban hell
(with Co-Op, tea shop, Globe Hotel)
is just too busy, far too racey
(He hangs out at Bovey Tracey)

But here we are, to celebrate
the two big birthdays of our mates –
One has stacked up half a ton,
the other one is fifty-one.
The juvenile, of course, is Knightley –
(always seems to get off lightly).

All this time they've earned a living
playing their guitars and singing,
First in pubs at an early stage
(before the legal drinking age)
And with the help of Mr. Downes
they learnt some songs and did the rounds
But even overwhelmed with praise
these likely lads went separate ways

With Stones, Old fields and Al-bi-on
Phil fiddled, picked and morrised on
While Steve sought fame in London's bars, he
soon found out that most were khazis –
Took to hovels, squatted flats
and teaching future media brats

Other schemes to make a bob
could not replace an honest job
Phil couldn't build or clean or cook
But what he knew could fill a book.
No amount of years at college
could improve Phil's local knowledge.
In hiking boots and sturdy kecks
he'd walked every inch of the River Exe.
No-one could come close I doubt,
He knows Devon inside out
But would his book remain unread:
"The ABC of the Exe-wise head"?

Due to lack of interest, Steve
packed up teaching, moved back west
Tried his hand at B&B
and C, Gr, F and D
He kept this going up until
he got some local gigs with Phil.

Soon enough they felt the pangs
for Groupies, cider, transit vans
So thinking we were short of bands
the boys created Show Of Hands
Knightley talked Phil into it
with rhetoric and ready wit:
"Before we reach too old an age
let's put our show on a bigger stage...
It should be a doddle this –
Verse/chorus/fiddle? Piece of piss"

So over one too many jars
They hatched a plan to tour the bars
filled with yokels pissed as newts
Plying them with folk and roots,
Regaling them with rural yarns
In function rooms, converted barns
Waking up on strangers' floors
A thousand curries on a hundred tours.
...Clubs and pubs, but best of all
The Glastonbury Festival

where scattered showers of drops and drips
turned into the Apocalypse.
But they got through the flood unscathed –
split the fifty quid and bathed.
Checked out flights they could afford
and vowed to take their sound abroad
as far away as they could reach –
Bremen! Bombay! Bondi Beach!
And selling records, if you please
(just 2 singles, twelve LPs)

They set about the task with gumption
(doubling UK fuel consumption)
Entertained the growing hordes
from Ibiza to the Norfolk Broads
(thank you David)
On motorways, in cars and trucks
they covered Tyneside, Hants and Bucks,
Trading songs for beer and grub in:
Looe, Hoo, Farningham, Crewe,
Southern and Midland clubs

They perpetrate this Carry-on
on tour and showofhandsdotcom
Still enjoying their careers
despite the fast advancing years.
And even when they take a break
they musically collaborate.
Some might say they just can't stay off the
2-4-6-8 motorway

A miracle they've come this far
(especially in Philip's car)
But Royal Albert goes to show
that giant oaks from acorns grow.

It's still some time before they can
expect the royal telegram,
But raise your glasses if you will –
Here's to Stephen! Here's to Phil!

MAY BANK HOLIDAY 2004

2010: **Covers 2**

Ten years on from Covers, Show of Hands again acknowledge the music that inspires them in this eclectic selection that includes songs they perform live.

2011: **Backlog 2**

Show of Hands recorded this set of songs voted for by their fans. They could choose any that they liked that first had an airing between 1992 and 2003.

STEVE: *"I don't know what Phil thinks about recording but I love it. It's like showing off in a nice little environment. I've been in all sorts of recording environments over the years and when someone says 'Sing it in an angry way' or 'Sing it in a funny way' or 'Sing it quietly' or 'What about singing it as if you can't remember the words', I enjoy the challenge of all that...*
...We've got to a very good position in the last 10 or so years with Mark Tucker who will capture what we do live but add studio polish to it, so it's a very interactive process. We're here in Devon, it's close, it's just available, Phil's got his own little room next door, so it's a very enjoyable process. If someone says 'We need a lyric in 5 minutes, go away and write it', I enjoy that. It's like passing tests. It's like a little quiz you've solved, whereas Phil has a different approach."

2012: **Wake The Union**

Produced by the band with old mate Mark Tucker and perfectly described by Show of Hands as "where Route 66 meets the A303," Wake The Union celebrates English and American roots music in an exploration of narrative themes that speak to us all. Following hot on the heels of Knightley's participation in a project that explored Cecil Sharp's song collecting career across the Atlantic, here he picks up the threads of historical connections between English and American folk. The album alternates an "American track" and an "English track" with instrumentation such as BJ Cole's pedal steel guitar providing musical motifs redolent with place. Covering Richard Shindell's Civil War epic Reunion Hill, the band acknowledge the American singer-songwriter whom they invited on tour, in a rare step for Show of Hands who generally swerve the singer-songwriter genre:

"It's people singing 'I live this elevated singer songwriter life of the road and transient relationships. But out there (in the audience) there might be someone who's dragged someone out of a car crash, or a single mother raising kids. Out there there's probably more tales of bravery than a lot of those singer songwriters could ever muster up. 'I was in Texas, I've lived my life.' (Beer sings: 'I was so lonely in my hotel room.') 'I'm going to give you examples of how I've lived my life.' I've never liked that. It's only redeemed by the absolute excellence of someone like Richard. If you were brought up immersed in the tradition, which to an extent I was with Carthy and Sidmouth and all that, you get a sense of the politics and the history so you don't tend to go down that route, you use characters to tell a story."

The tales on Wake The Union, including the opening track co-written with Seth Lakeman, run the gamut of human emotion, from desolation to joy. And joy defined the album's general media reception. It even reached no.35 at one point in the UK midweek album charts.

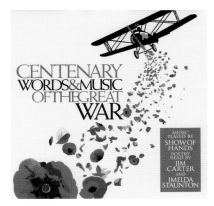

Left: Steve at Abbey Road Studios with Jim Carter and Imelda Staunton during their poetry readings for Centenary

2014: Centenary (Words & Music of the Great War).

Disc one featured classic Great War poems read by old friends Jim Carter and Imelda Staunton set to subtle and moving instrumental music. Disc Two presented original and traditional material inspired by the War. The album's graceful commemoration encapsulated the public mood for remembrance. Here Knightley's talent for conflating time as he brings history slap-bang back into the present gives the album a timeless relevance. Produced by Mark Tucker and Steve Knightley, the music was recorded in Devon and the narration at Abbey Road, London. Released on Ian Brown's Mighty Village Label via Universal, the album received critical and public acclaim, going straight to no. 13 in the compilation album charts, securing widespread radio play and landing the band back on the Andrew Marr show. The 2016 performance of Centenary in Exeter Cathedral added a haunting resonance to the music.

PHIL: *" Now, it's not like the old days with great big spaces with sound booths in recording studios where 'bands' can play together, it just doesn't quite work that way any more, although those studios are still around. In fact the silliness of both 'Dark Fields' and 'Lie of the Land' is with us being down at Joe Partridge's, which is a monstrous old-fashioned space, rattling around in a building the size of a small church just playing acoustic guitar and thinking 'this is all a bit silly.'"*

PHIL: "Recording is an entirely different process now. We're often not in the same place at the same time any more because I hate hanging around, I can't stand twiddling my thumbs while other people are doing stuff, it just bores me to tears. Generally speaking if there is no live template, no performance template, it's best if Steve concentrates on his guitar playing and putting a voice down and then we tend to have a chat about what's going to go with it. Then I will come in with this set-up here (at Mark Tucker's sound studio) where I've got Mark's old room, I can go next door and start buggering around with my set-up while they're working on something else…"

2016: **The Long Way Home**

"As it sort of implies there's a bit more actual folk music here than there has been for a while. The bottom line was a return to the songs that inspired us when we met. So there's a large dose of those, including a version of the West Country song "Twas On One April's Morning' that Tony Rose – a regular on the Exeter folk scene when Beer and Knightley were setting out – made his own." Partly recorded in Phil Beer's studio and completed at The Green Room and produced once more by the band and Mark Tucker. Show of Hands look back to their early days as a duo, bringing the insights of their extraordinary and prolific career to vivid musical life. It's a pared down sound, more duo than trio and more Devonian than American. And yet as one might expect from Knightley and Beer, men who've spent a lifetime looking out to sea, the songs refer to wider horizons: Mesopotamia, for example, uses the Napoleonic War tradition of tales of girls going off to join their soldier lovers to refer to girls now travelling to Syria to become Jihadi brides. Again receiving both critical and popular acclaim, the album secured Show of Hands' first top ten chart placing – pleasing but not fundamental to the band, to whom gigging and connecting live with their audience as they've done right from the start is still the thing that matters most.

STEVE: *"It's a question of saying 'OK, what stories, what topics, what subject matters, what titles have you put aside'. Currently I've got one that I've had for a while called 'No Secrets' which came out of me giving Seth some advice when he got married. Everyone had to give him a piece of advice and mine was 'have no secrets, not one, not a little cupboard anywhere, simply that if you have one secret you'll add another to it and another and another and another."*

Above: Phil backstage at Hastings
PHIL: *"On every record there'll be something that's recorded on an iPhone. There's an awful lot of that."*
Left and opposite: Steve with Mark Tucker in his studio 'The Green Room'
Top: The Long Way Home album cover, Seth Lakeman, Jim Causley and Jackie Oates contributing to various Show of Hands projects

2005

✤ Appearance at Celtic Connections

✤ Steve Knightley toured with Martyn Joseph
– their album The Bridgerow Sessions is released

✤ Another 'Up Close' Tour

✤ July 9th – The band's annual outdoor event at
Abbotsbury features guests including Spiers & Boden
and compere Les Barker

✤ They squeeze in 15 festival appearances during
Spring and Summer

✤ 'As You Were' Autumn Tour

✤ September – live dates in Germany and The Netherlands

✤ Miranda has become a permanent fixture on
Show of Hands live dates

"SHOW OF HANDS"
at
Cropredy Village Hall
on
Saturday, 4th June 2005
at 8.00 p.m.

£14.00   Licensed Bar
              Doors open at 7.00 p.m.

7.30

SIDMOUTH FolkW
29 July - 5 August 20

concerts ceilidhs morris sessions workshops dances child

Bellowhead • Show of H
Battlefield Band • Kathryn Tickell
Whapweasel • Last Night's
The Hush • Jez Lowe & The Bad Pe
Bismarcks • Random • Little Johnny Eng
John Kirkpatrick • Brendan Power with Tim Edey & Lucy
Martyn Wyndham-Read & Iris Bishop • Harvey An
TrioTHRELFALL • Damien Barber • Strav
New Scorpion Band • Dr Faustus • Patterson Jordan D
Alison McMorland & Geordie Mc
Hot Rats • Craig: Morgan: Robson • Moor M
Emily Portman & Lauren McCormick • Jim Ca
Nandobinyan • Beltaine • Rhyzome • Dave V
Bonsai Band • Hannah & the Madding C
The Blackfoot Brothers • All Jigged Out • Grand U
Thingamijig • Blackthorn • Joe le Taxi • Mr St
Mick Brooks • Baz Parkes • Ed Rennie • Jackie O
Gwilym Davies • Keith Kendrick • Sylvia Needl
Jim & Bev James • Nick & Mary Barber • Eddie Up
Paul Burgess • Derek Schofield • Pendragon • Stradivarie
Kelly's Eye • Newfolk • High Jinks • Orion's Ri
Hobson's Choice • Charles Bolton • Colin Hume • Chris Turn
Mike Courthold • Geoff Cubitt • Frances Oates • Robert Mo
Gerry Yates • Anne Welch • Valerie Webster • Ron Rud
Rosemary Hunt • Ivan Aitken • Carrie Atkinso
Janet Dowling • West Gallery Music Association
West Country Concertina Players • Sidmouth Steppers
Black Swan Rapper • Fabulous Fezheads
Ladies of the Rolling Pin (Rhode Island USA)
... and lots more to come!

Yes – it's happening! For the latest news visit
www.sidmouthfolkweek.co.uk
or write to Sidmouth FolkWeek, Tourist Information Centre, Sidmouth, Devon EX10 8XR

March / April 2005

Steve Knightle
KNIGHTLE

Tonbridge School
Spyboy Promotions
Show Of Hands

Saturday 28 May, 2005   08:00pm
Stalls   Row E   Seat 2

Price 0.00   Complimentary
School Grounds
Please note parking is not permitted in the
school grounds this evening
Tonbridge Services Limited Licensed bar opens 7.15pm

Martyn
Joseph   Presents
                        Show of Hands
                Sat, 19 February 2005

Balcony   Row R Seat 15
Adult/Full Price   £ 0.00

theBROADWA
Latecomers may not be admitted
Forester Theatre
BOX OFFICE 020 8507 560
visit us at www.thebroadwaybarking.co

STEVE: *"I always know what Phil is going to do next, but I don't know why."*
Photoshoot for the Witness album,
Spitalfields, London 2006

"I can't read or write a note. But that visualisation, It's odd that I was doing that before I could play."

2006

❖ Spring Tour

❖ SOH are asked to contribute a track to a Beatles tribute album – Rubber Folk is a complete album of covers of the Rubber Soul album

❖ The band record If I Needed Someone, which is coupled with the title track Witness on a single release

❖ Witness is released – produced by Simon Emmerson and Mass of Afro Celt Sound System, and assisted by SOH sound man Mick Dolan

❖ 'Witness' Autumn Tour with Martyn Joseph as support

❖ In August the band visit Canada to play the Canmore, Vermillion and Edmonton Festivals

❖ Merchandise manager Kevin Henderson and sound man Mick Dolan both leave the crew for pastures new

"There's a great quote: someone said that I build the house and Phil decorates it. But they're not always there when the work's being done! The other thing Phil says is 'I've gone to Bermuda'. It means mentally he's left, he's standing there doing what he does but he's left the building. And he can go to Bermuda at any time, even in the middle of a meeting, he's just gone, Elvis has left the building."

"You once said if you don't use it you'll wake one day and find it gone"

THE HARVEST YEARS

The success of Witness with it's rhythmically sensuous AfroCelt cool drew in a new WOMAD audience to Show of Hands, who performed at the festival for the first time in 2008 along with a further 22 festivals that year. This had a positive impact on raising Show of Hands profile with people that wouldn't normally see them, but Beer and Knightley were still finding they had to overcome preconceptions of them that were essentially negative. Hearing over and over again "I don't like folk, but I like you!" Or echoing O'Farrell years before, "If I'd known it was you, I wouldn't have bothered wandering over." ("But am glad I did")

Part of this is because non-folk audiences have an idea of folk that is generally not based on being informed about the music or its breadth, whilst traditional folk audiences tend to see any change or innovation as 'Americanisation' or 'going commercial'. The perception is that while either of those tendencies might not be heretical, they are certainly 'not folk'. Difficult then for Show of Hands who are entirely up-front about their influences (2012's Wake The Union is where "Route 66 meets the A303"). Beer and Knightley might not have folk music in their biological DNA, removing their backstage pass to the artists' dressing room as far as traditionalists are concerned, but it's certainly a dominant gene in their musical make-up.

MIRANDA: "...Steve comes across as arrogant but he is not very self-confident in many ways. He is constantly on edge but he puts on this facade of arrogance which just isn't true! He is actually one of the most considerate people I know. He reads people: he is a typical artist."
...Phil, he's one of the most generous people, he is a complete darling and lives in a crazy world. He is super, super talented and it never ceases to amaze me that he can just pick up an instrument. Steve will say: 'try that on fiddle' and 'try that on blah' and he just 'diddle diddle diddle dah' and plays it away. And I think: 'how the hell do you just do that?' He's amazing! I don't know how he just bimbles through life as he does, spinning so many plates."
Opposite and left: On stage at WOMAD 2008, Phil in Peterborough 2016, Miranda in Leicester 2007

Greatest Devonians

Whilst immersed in English and particularly West Country tradition they use instruments from other traditions to express essentially English tales. Instinctively they paint with the vivid colours of a wider musical palette that, along with American and Latin American roots music, includes Gaelic and Indian classical textures too. All these influences seamlessly blend in their sound as they spring from their life experiences. The English they say, have always been pirates, taking on board the food and literature of other cultures. "We just do it with music".

This would have been lost on the one-time Under Secretary of State for Culture, Media and Sport - Kim Howells who in 2001 infamously summed up the non-folk view saying: "the idea of listening to three Somerset folk singers sounds like hell," prompting Show of Hands' riposte in the stomping Witness track Roots. The song attracted a whole new audience, though this was not to be the positive experience that the band might reasonably have expected. Though Roots called for unity in diversity, in a woeful misinterpretation of the lyrics the BNP posted it up as a rallying call. Beer and Knightley had to wrench their track down from the BNP website. They then helped launch Folk Against Fascism, and gave roots to the movement's eponymous debut double album released in 2010.

Right: Show of Hands most popular album to date.
Above: Unused designs for the Roots album
Above, right: Show of Hands as illustrated by Brian Lewis following the news that Steve and Phil had beaten Sir Francis Drake into second place in a regional BBC poll to ascertain the 'Greatest Devonions'

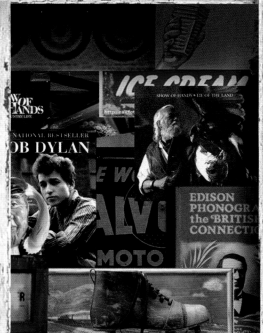

ROOTS

THE BEST OF *Est.* 1991

SHOW of HANDS

YOUR COLOURS THE MAST

For Show of Hands breaking down misconceptions in order to reach a wider audience is like treading through a minefield – pleasing one set of people always risks alienating another. But on the follow-up to Witness, a double album also called Roots, (2007) they reached out to their core audience who were asked to vote for their favourite Show of Hands track to date and the winning titles appeared on the second CD.

2009's Arrogance, Ignorance And Greed with it's direct lyrics such as "You're on your yacht/We're on our knees/With your arrogance and ignorance and greed" on the title track, created a current that carried them into the mainstream as they nailed the bankers to their mast and voiced the public's anger in anthemic song. Stuart Hanna's raw production captured the prevailing mood and the album gained widespread national radio airplay, garnered brilliant reviews across the mainstream press and earned the band a spot on the Andrew Marr Show. The accompanying guerrilla-filmed video features huge images of Beer, Knightley and Sykes performing the song projected high on to City of London banks as monkey masked graffiti artists work Banksy style below. It went viral on YouTube. Touring the album, Show of Hands won Best Duo at 2010's BBC Folk Awards with Arrogance Ignorance and Greed also winning the gong for Best Song.

Opposite: Stills from the video shoot for Arrogance, Ignorance and Greed

ROB O'CONNOR on Arrogance, Ignorance, and Greed: *"Driving back from a lunchtime roadside pub meeting with Steve, Phil and Vaughan somewhere halfway between Kent and Devon, I was mentally revisiting the visual concepts I'd just shown them for AIG, wondering how we'd not quite managed to visually encapsulate the powerful message of the album's title track. Stylorouge colleague Mark Higenbottam and I had created a dozen or more concepts to present, and we were acutely aware that we were asking Show of Hands to make quite a departure from their normal imagery. We wanted to express the horror and tragedy of what money – and in particular the so-called banking crisis – had inflicted on the common man and woman; the avarice, the blood-letting, the filthy lucre, the camouflaged criminality of our esteemed establishment. My conclusion was that the visual language needed to be more direct, more political, but delivered with a modicum of anarchic mischief...*

SHOW of HANDS

ARROGANCE IGNORANCE AND GREED

"...The tedium of the M25 must have triggered a brainstorm — an image of three not-so-wise monkeys popped into my head, and after getting a phonecall thumbs-up from Steve, we pursued this route.

As with Country Life, the band agreed to doing a video for the title track too — Steve's original suggestion was to document the band performing the song busking-style to passing bankers in either the City of London or Canary Wharf, where they would almost certainly have been moved on before the end of the first chorus, so we hatched a more complicated (and expensive) plot to project live footage of them (filmed in the gig room at Gibson Guitars headquarters) alongside political slogans and graphics of the monkeys onto the walls of these same financial strongholds. This exercise turned into a dramatised full-on fake guerrilla campaign, also involving flyposting and media-hacked video billboards.

The overnight film shoot was almost scuppered at the first hurdle, when our small crew was surrounded by Police riot vans as soon as the projector was turned on outside the Bank Of England. Fortunately sanity prevailed and we were allowed to move on (unbeknown to the constabulary only to our next projection location). The campaign was pulled together back in the relative safety of our East London studio by Mark Higenbottam and editor Jamie Gibson and we were able to incorporate some great shots of city workers leaving offices and drinking and eating 'at every trough' in the square mile, which keyboard maestro Matt Clifford had garnered from a previous night's filming foray into the City. (Matt has also filmed a lot of other Show of Hands material — his video for Roots has been an unqualified YouTube success).
The resulting visual campaign for Arrogance, Ignorance & Greed felt like a fitting accompaniment to the key tracks on the album, and in particular to Stu Hanna's spontaneously spiky production..."

Opposite: Unused visuals for the album artwork

PHIL: *"There's a hard core who constantly moan about new songs and then they eventually love them. Again, I don't want to break the chronology, one of the last four albums alienated the hard core so much because it was quite different from what we'd done before, and yet ironically was the best reviewed...*
...It was 'AIG' (Arrogance, Ignorance and Greed). It's simply that we had a young, smart producer who has a very dry, crisp way of presenting things. Even we weren't sure of how the album sounded but it just got the reviewers' attention."

Above and Left: The photoshoot for Arrogance, Ignorance and Greed was located at Morewelham Industrial Heritage site on the banks of the Taymar, to evoke a sense of the Industrial Revolution

Whilst the album's success helped to draw in a wider audience who did not identify with a particular tribe (in part due to the new ways people were listening and 'liking' music of every genre via the internet), AIG took a while to win round some members of their core community who missed the smooth production and subtle metaphors in the historical narratives that were familiar to them. Whilst the follow-up release Covers 2 (2010) pointed to the duos diverse more mainstream influences, Backlog 2 the following year resulted from the bands direct collaboration with their core audience. Communicating via their Longdogs fanclub web forum, people voted for their favourite Show of Hands songs from 1991-2003. Beer, Knightley and Sykes recorded each track as if live, delivering the immediacy and intimacy of that experience back again to the people who'd been with them since they'd begun.

2007

✤ Spring Tour

✤ The third Royal Albert Hall concert takes place

✤ Steve releases Cruel River, his second solo album

✤ He also produces a solo album for Devon singer/songwriter Jenna – recorded by Phil at the band's Riverside Studio

✤ Steve produces Jez Lowe's solo album

✤ SOH play the Eden Project session, supporting Peter Gabriel

✤ Steve hosts a songwriting session at Womad Summer Festival and at Peter Gabriel's invitation they sing a couple of songs at the BMI Music Awards where Peter receives the prestigious 'Icon' award

✤ Phil and Steve are made patrons of Trowbridge Village Pump Festival, and Shrewsbury is the year's highlight

✤ Miranda joins Phil for his 'solo' tour with guests alternating between shows; Jackie Oates, Isambarde and Mawkin

✤ A record-breaking (by SOH standards) seventeen Summer/festival gigs

✤ Steve's third songbook is published

✤ Designer Brad Waters comes on board to maintain the Show of Hands website

✤ Roots, The Best Of Show of Hands is released as a double album. All the tracks on CD 2 of the double set are selected by Longdogs...

✤ 'Backlog' duo Autumn Tour for SOH, showcasing old favourite songs

✤ September dates in Germany
SOH Tour with Slaid Cleeves as support and Miranda rejoining, but at short notice Steve is forced to pull out of the tour

✤ Steve and Clare Knightley's oldest son, Jack is taken ill with Leukaemia

Hey Steve + Phil –
I actually really enjoyed your CD but moved shortly after receiving it am just recently rediscovered it. [...] for the pathetic delay in letting you know I mean it!

best wishes,

Natalie Merchant

STEVE KNIGHTLEY SONGBOOK 3

SHOW OF HANDS ROOTS *made into* COUNTRY LIFE
"Steve Knightley's songs have developed such an edge that [...] hard to deny them any longer" – Colin Irwin (Mojo)

31 ORIGINAL SONGS FROM COUNTRY LIFE, WITNESS AND CRUEL RIVER

PHIL BEER THE SOLO TOUR 2007
with Miranda Sykes

LONGDOGS

SHOW OF HANDS

Door
Loggia

Seat

Sun, 08 April 2007
At 7:30 PM
Doors open at 6:45 PM

Account No 458016

£28.00

2314116 1a 3 SHSH01

STEVE KNIGHTLEY CRUEL RIVER

STEVE ON PHIL: *"Phil's life is totally different from mine in terms of responsibility and commitments. From the moment he wakes up to the moment he goes to bed he can choose what he does, there is no-one tugging his sleeve, apart from when he had to look after his mum and dad in the latter years. Apart from that he sets the agenda for his days and what he wishes to do which is very different from mine."*

Opposite: Unused sleeve designs for
the Wake The Union album
Words Can Be Weapons was an early
working title

2008

❖ A single is taken from the Witness album – Roots is promoted with a promo video and the track causes quite a stir on social media

❖ SOH hit the road for a Spring Tour

❖ Steve co-writes three songs on Seth Lakeman's album "Poor Man's Heaven"

❖ Jenna supports Steve on his solo tour

❖ Overseas gigs are put on hold this year due to Jack's illness, but the band get stuck into a variety of different UK gigs

❖ 'Spires and Beams' Tour takes in cathedrals and historic buildings

❖ 'Standing Room Only' is a standing Autumn Tour with Ruarri Joseph as support, and 23(!) festival appearances include the band's first ever WOMAD

❖ Show of Hands fans continue to send warm messages of support as Jack Knightley continues to undergo treatment for his illness

❖ Longdogs celebrates its 10th anniversary as SOH's official independent 'fan club'

❖ Phil is on a weight-loss programme, making money for charity in the process. He's also preparing for next years Tall Ships race in which he will take part

❖ Phil also releases albums by Jackie Oates and the late Tony Rose on his own Chudleigh Roots label

Original manager Gerard O'Farrell had returned to Australia in 2001 when Vaughan and subsequently Gwen Pearce stepped in. (Friends since the band had played in the folk club the couple ran in Amersham, Vaughan had for some time been touring with Show of Hands, having taken charge of the merchandising). The cottage industry inspired and implemented by O'Farrell was burgeoning. Vaughan enjoyed dealing with the agency side of the business, whilst Gwen, with her distribution background and top job at Warners/Sony, took over the reins at the Hands On Music label.

The Pearces understood that the key to Show of Hands increasing success was their fundamental interconnection with their core audience and recognition of that importance by the band – even if at times (as in the case of AIG), Beer, Knightley and Sykes' realisation of their creative inspiration sidestepped their fans expectations.

Top: Backstage at Yeovil, October 2008
Above: Vaughan and Gwen Pearce
sharing managerial duties at
Abbotsbury in 2015

- ❖ Spring Tour

- ❖ Longdogs raise £8,000 towards the fund to expedite Jack Knightley's treatment for Leukaemia

- ❖ 'County Towns' Autumn Tour

- ❖ Steve joins fellow musicians in launching Folk Against Fascism

- ❖ Phil and his fellow crew of the good ship Pegasus celebrate coming second in the Tall Ships race (and first in her class)

- ❖ Steve and Friends run Abbotsbury in Phil's absence. Port Isaac Fisherman's Friends are on the bill

- ❖ Arrogance, Ignorance & Greed is released, produced by Megson's Stu Hanna

- ❖ A video is made for the title track – political graphics and performance footage of Steve, Phil and Miranda are projected on the Bank Of England and other financial buildings in the City of London

- ❖ Steve re-records the album Track Of Words and released "Track Of Words – Retraced" in May 2009

- ❖ The "County Towns" Tour kicks off in September – Franco/Geordie singer/guitarist Flossie Malavialle support

SUMMER FAMILY CONCERT
ABBOTSBURY July 4th 2009

Running order

STEVE KNIGHTLEY introducing

JENNA 3.00-3.45

MAWKIN:CAUSLEY 4.00-4.45

MIRANDA SYKES 5.00-5.45

INTERVAL - 5.45-6.15

FISHERMEN'S FRIENDS 6.15-7.00

MARTYN JOSEPH 7.10-7.55

STEVE KNIGHTLEY & FRIENDS 8.00-9.00

SHOW OF HANDS with MIRANDA SYKES
TOUR DATES 2009

Available now ROOTS THE BEST OF SHOW OF HANDS
The definitive collection. A 2 CD set with 30 re-mastered tracks including 4 new recordings of concert favourites 'Are We Alright', 'Exile', 'Santiago' and 'Crow on the Cradle'.
Available from all good record stores or online at www.showofhands.co.uk

SHOW OF HANDS
with MIRANDA SYKES
TOUR DATES 2009

FEBRUARY
Sat 14 'FOLKPORT'   01704 540011
SOUTHPORT Arts Centre 'Day of Folk'

MARCH
Sun 8 BURGESS HILL   01444 242888
'Fairtrade & Freedom Festival 2009'
Wed 18 to Sun 29 GERMANY

APRIL
Fri 10 GOSPORT & FAREHAM   01329 231942
Easter Festival
Wed 15 MAIDENHEAD Norden Farm AC   01628 788997
Thu 16 SHREWSBURY Theatre Severn   01743 281281
Fri 17 SALTAIRE Victoria Hall   01274 588614
Sat 18 BURNLEY Mechanics   01282 664400
Sun 19 SALFORD The Lowry   0870 787 5780
Wed 22 WESTON-SUPER-MARE   01934 645544
The Playhouse
Thu 23 STROUD Subscription Rooms   01453 760900
Fri 24 KENDAL Brewery Arts Centre 01539 725133
Sat 25 GATESHEAD   0191 443 4661
The Sage Gateshead
Sun 26 HULL Albemarle Music Centre 01482 226655
(Hull City Hall)
0845 293 8480
Wed 29 BATH Komedia (Komedia Brighton box office)
Thu 30 MILFORD HAVEN Torch Theatre 01646 695267

Sun 10 LONDON   020 7388 8822
UCL Bloomsbury Theatre 0845 094 5423
Wed 13 FOWEY   0151 666 0000
Daphne du Maurier Festival
Thu 14 BIRKENHEAD Pacific Road AC 01246 345222
Fri 15 CHESTERFIELD Winding Wheel (Pomegranate Theatre)
SWAVESEY Spring Festival 01484 222444 (TIC)
Sun 17 EXMOUTH Pavilion   01395 222477
(RNLI fund raiser)   01872 512466
Sun 30 MARLBOROUGH COLLEGE
Memorial Hall,
Marlborough Folk Roots
10th Anniversary concert

JUNE   01443 485934
Wed 3 PONTYPRIDD
Muni Arts Centre   01684 295074
Thu 4 TEWKESBURY
The Roses Theatre   0151 647 0752
Fri 5 WIRRAL   01630 816878
Folk on the Coast Festival
Sat 6 SOUTHWELL   01484 582900
'Gate to Southwell Folk Festival'
Sun 7 CHESHAM The Elgiva Theatre 01342 302000
Fri 19 EAST GRINSTEAD
Chequer Mead Arts Centre 023 9282 8722
(Festival)
Sat 20 PORTSMOUTH Festivities
New Theatre Royal   023 9264 9000
(Theatre)

JULY   01305 871130
Sat 4 ABBOTSBURY
Sub-Tropical Gardens
Summer Family Concert
Line up includes STEVE KNIGHTLEY,
MAWKIN:CAUSLEY,

01239 621200

This page: Show of Hands' popularity amongst their fanbase finally won them a BBC Folk Award in 2004 when they were voted Best Live Act.
The following year they were nominated the Best Duo and won Best Group award as part of Oyster Band Big Session Group.
In February 2010 they won Best Duo and Best Original Song for Arrogance, Ignorance and Greed

STEVE: "Just because someone has no sense of time-keeping, they're never early, which is interesting because you'd think they'd be late as often as they're early but they're always late."

Main picture: Photo opportunity in the sunlit Haldon Belvedere Tower near Exeter, 2015

without stories, without songs, how
will we know where we've come from"
WRITING THE SONGS

STEVE: *"I met Ted Hughes and he re-wired me personally, face-to-face."*

I'd known things like 'The Horses' and 'Pike' and 'The Thought Fox' and I was always impressed with the muscularity of his writing. But when I was 15, and this was in the C stream of the Grammar school, the English teacher read out that there was this creative writing course at the Arvon Foundation in Beaford. So we went off to Beaford Manor in North Devon to this wonderful old vicarage and, far from just hanging out and drinking all week, which is what our plan was, I actually bought into it. They would give you a notebook and say 'This morning you're going to go down to the river and you're just going to write down everything you can see'. So I started sketching out these things. I remember one about 'The wind will never free you, pebbles underwater, but it tries though with fingers of something across the water's surface'. I remember writing down this stuff and these guys were saying 'This is really quite good Steve'. And I thought Wow, I write poetry ".

I hadn't really started writing songs at that point, a little bit, but after three or four days of this I'd got quite into it, unlike my friends who were just dutifully doing the right things. Then on the final night John Fairfax said 'Ted Hughes is going to come and read to us by the fireside and you are going to read whatever stuff you've created during the week and Ted Hughes will...' And this extraordinary man came in, a big northern bloke, looked like Freddie Truman, big gruff voice. He read stuff from 'Crow', 'Blood, the guts, tumbling, trembling featherless elbows in the nest's filth', really brutal stuff. Then we had to do our stuff and I strummed a little song and read some stuff."

"Afterwards he came up to me and said 'What's your name son?'. And I said 'Steve Knightley'. He said 'No, no, what's your full name?'. I said 'Steven Andrew Knightley'. He said 'The Celts would say if you gave a man your full name he had your soul. Now I've got yours'. And he went like 'that' with his hands, like he was catching a fly, and he just walked away and spoke to someone else. I recently asked Michael Morpurgo, old friend of Ted Hughes and author of War Horse, 'Have you heard that story before?', and he said 'No, that was just for you'. So then I went away and read everything by Ted Hughes, and also George Barker and George Macbeth and Louis MacNeice, I read all of that generation of poets and I think that was the final ingredient, after the Dylan stuff and after Martin Carthy, that was the final ingredient in the way I wanted to write songs. It's only looking back that you realise that you're at a crossroads like that."

"When I first met Clare I read to her one of Hughes' rare emotional poems, and I've never read a love poem to someone over the phone before, I forget the actual phrase now but I learned that poem. I think it's called 'Oh My Lady'.
O lady, when the tipped cup of the moon blessed you
You became soft fire with a cloud's grace;
... and so on... I memorised it and I sneaked off and found a phone box and recited it. I thought that would

STEVE: *"You can't lose sight of what it is most people do for a living and how lucky you are to be able to benefit from the fruits of that in order to support your lifestyle."*

STEVE: *"When I lived in Dorset I met this extraordinary intellectual called Philip Rawson, who was one of the world's leading authorities on Indian art. He came to a gig and we were supported by a guy, another singer/songwriter, and Philip said 'I couldn't bear that man. You have a poetic sensibility and that guy doesn't have a shred'. And I'd never heard that expression used, a poetic sensibility. And now I recognise that. I know lots of very, very fine musicians who don't have that. It's not a thread in their music. It's quite rare, actually, you can get a long way as a songwriter and a lot of people fake it, they fake it with abstract words and they fake it with incoherent lyrics, and they think there's a poetic sensibility running through it. There has to be an inner truth that you know and you can justify and account for at any one time. I'm not sure every revered rock star has got that. But you spot it, and Philip spotted it in me. Maybe Ted Hughes did, I don't know.*

I'm drawn to intellectuals, I like the way they think. Phil doesn't spot them, that's not his world. People like James Studholme and an amazing guy I met called John Bush who think abstractly or think outside the box, who see the patterns behind things and who recognise the patterns within what you do, that's an intellectual and an abstract way of looking at behaviour."

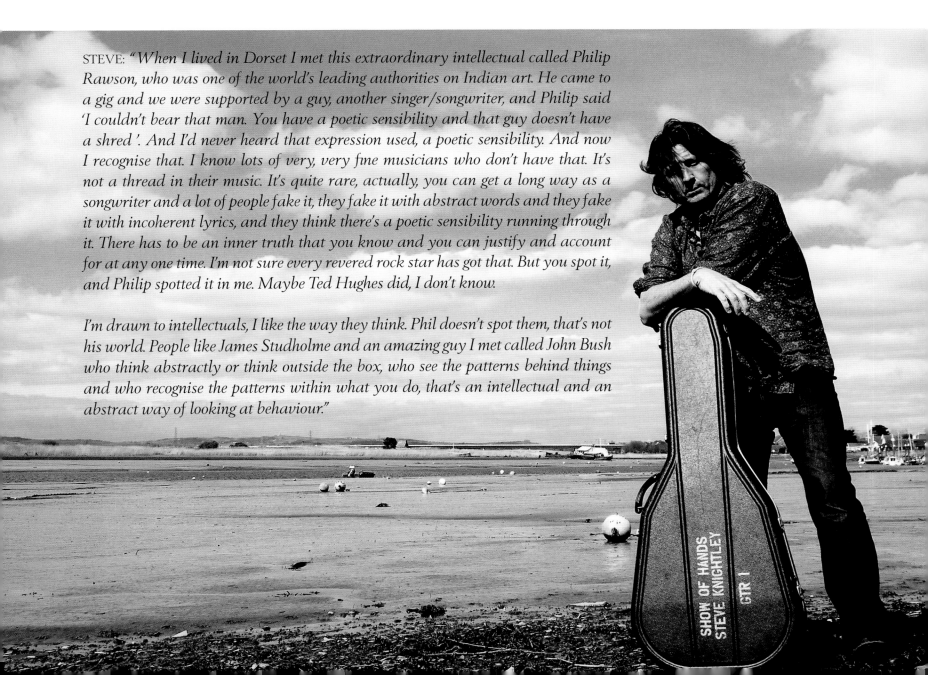

STEVE: *"The favourite song is the one that you're currently writing, and the next one, and you tend to think that it's the best one ever in order to have the front to play it to people. I have some that I'm very proud of the poetry of, I think 'Exile' is very good 'Waves breaking far at sea', I really like a song called 'Hook of Love' – 'There's a hook of love beneath her skin, the harder she pulls away the deeper it goes in' - I like that image. 'The Dive' is very poetic. So there are songs that I'm very proud of the lyrics but I don't particularly have a favourite...*

...I wrote Exile when I was teaching in London. There were some girls in the class from Eritrea, the most exquisitely beautifully defined faces, very black skin, like Iman, faces like that. They were so quiet and so far from home. Noticing all the other people in London: dispossessed, Palestinians, Eritreans, whatever, in the mid-'80s, I just wrote a song 'Exile' which I think Phil now sings. It was always one of his favourites and he makes a joke about it: "There was one particular song I liked" and I always respond saying "Just the one then?". But I think he probably saw in that song the possibility of others that would get a response on the scene that he was familiar with...

'Santiago' is always requested and so is 'Cousin Jack'. It's the song that accords with our basic sound and principles. It's about emigration, family and belonging, it's a song about knowing your past, about having a relationship with an occupation that defines you. It's also about trying to find a voice with which to express yourself. So people who are from all parts of the world come up and say that song touched them. Melodically and lyrically it is the song that must connect to our audience the most, they see themes in it that they relate to. 'Cousin Jack' is probably the most well-known song that I've written, particularly in the West Country."

PHIL: *"My Great Aunt Polly's husband' is Cousin Jack', John Lean, he went to the States in the '30s. In those days you could sign on to a ship, not get paid but it would get you to the States. As a non-sailor you could work your passage. He was a miner, he had just lost his job again, decided to go off to the States and make his fortune, and was never heard of again, as a lot of them did. They didn't make their fortunes, they didn't have any money to send home so a lot of them just married again and technically disappeared."*

STEVE: *"Everyone dreams of the time they write this lottery ticket song that takes them away from all this. And all their friends tell them about a friend of a friend who wrote a song that so-and-so. But I always say to musicians: 'There are no lottery ticket songs. All you've got is a trip to the shops, so you might as well make that a nice one, because there's nothing else."*

PHIL: *"'Santiago' is the one they really love. Oddly enough it's not 'Exile' for the people, that's for me really, that's a personal choice. 'Galway Farmer'. In recent years it's obviously been a couple of the more edgy political ones that they won't play on radio like 'Country Life' and 'Roots'...*

...The quote we had from the BBC with Country Life was literally 'This song is too issues-based for the daytime audience'. That's the BBC saying 'Our audience are a bit dumb'. But then there's this backdoor through which people who have absolute control over the little music that they play, like Andrew Marr and Jeremy Vine, who already like us, we get these astounding occasional plays from time to time. Simon Mayo has been incredibly good to us, but they're in absolute control of what they're doing, that's a whole different ball game. In fact, with his tongue in his cheek, Steve actually did this thing – the most innocuous and irrelevant song of the last album was the one that we put out on a single and it got playlisted! It was the one that mentions all the songs they won't play and that's the one that got playlisted."

"Despite the centralist to-left politics displayed in the stronger songs, to be honest I see them as just being social and observational, I think that's a good way of putting it."

MIRANDA: *"No Secrets' is just such a strong song and it is very personal to me because my love life has been a bit random and a bit chequered and finally I have found the love of my life. Steve and Phil were witnesses to my wedding and the song 'No Secrets' just is everything that Dan and I build our relationship on really. That one to me says everything in a song. Steve is often very poignant, he notices things, acknowledges things and that means a lot."*

STEVE: *"Phil has no agenda and not a political bone in his body. He will never gossip about other musicians. He will never think about 'How does that make me look?' or 'What can I get from that?' He doesn't blunder through life but he's on his own course. ...I always say I know what he'll do next, I don't know why, but I know what he'll do. So if I say to him 'Phil, can you play that on the violin', he's not going to think 'Oh, everyone likes me playing it on the violin, no I'm not', he'll say 'Yeah, alright, what do you want?' Or I'll say 'Phil, can you not even sing on that one' and he'll go 'Oh, OK'*

...There's a part of him that genuinely doesn't care, and I don't mean that in an unkind way. It's like the folk awards and all that acclaim and reviews, he genuinely doesn't care, and that's very, very rare in musicians. And what it does, it gives me free reign in a way. I can say to Phil 'Phil, you know that song you played the guitar on, can you go to the back of the room and hide?', and he'll go 'Yeah, alright'. He'll try anything out, he's very flexible like that."

Above: Steve on the photoshoot for his solo project Off The Beaten Track 2013,
Right: Probably Knightley's last handwritten lyrics prior to investing in a laptop,
Opposite: At Haldon Belvedere Tower

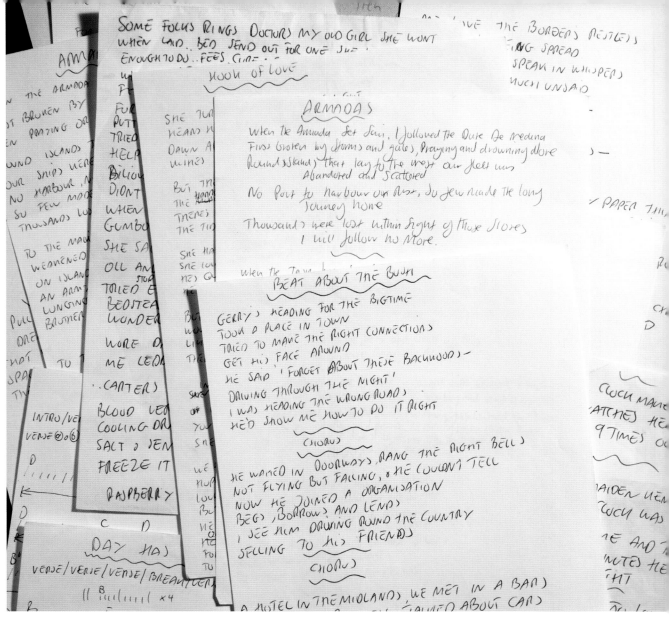

PHIL: *"Steve's standard of writing has maintained itself to a very, very high degree. At the end of the day it is what our audience are buying into, if that's the right expression to use. So even the thing of 'Oh I only like the old material' eventually moves aside for people liking stuff from the last four or five albums. It's just very important that that standard is maintained."*

"Exile', it's simply a song way ahead of its time. We've just started doing it again because it encapsulates everything about everything that's going on at this point in time."

STEVE: *"I've always known instinctively, unlike some other singer/songwriters, that you're looking at an audience where there are stories of courage and bravery and originality that you don't even know about. People might have been pulling someone out of a car crash that afternoon, there might be someone raising a disabled child, there might be someone leading a life of great bravery. And I've got to know so many pompous singer/songwriters over the years who talk about 'I was in a bar in Holland', it's almost like they lead this elevated life. And you hear that tone all the time 'Yeah, well the new album...', that self-important entitlement tone you get amongst some musicians. And I'd never bought that."*

With Facebook, this interactive process has become even more immediate. In September 2016, Knightley set out on his project to write a song a week for a month. For this he prosaically distilled his process into four types. "I thought, OK I write the American singer songwritery thing, I do the Irishy thing, I do the storytelling ballads and I do the big shouty AIG sort of songs. So I thought: Right I'll do one of each!" A narrative might spring from a news item or a passing comment, "You just made the right noises, didn't you?" Or a particular place. This might suggest a melody, or perhaps a pairing with a chord progression recorded on his phone one day as the muse struck. Knightley posted his workings on line and interwove the feedback into his work.

His love of history and politics informs Knightley's writing not just in the traditional style narrative ballads, but in his gimlet-eyed search for facts, whatever the subject. Neither he nor Beer can bear the false nostalgia that can muddy the lens of folk music. Show of Hands commemorate history and ties with place but you will not find them singing about the golden days of life down the mines or the pretty pastoral ease of agricultural life anytime soon.

STEVE: *"People would be surprised at some of my opinions, they would probably consider reactionary and quite conservative, because I don't think in terms of party politics, I just think I know what I believe to be true. I'm considered political but sometimes I think I would be considered too left or too right - I'm in favour of mass immigration, I think it's essential for a country. So there are contradictions. Living in the countryside I'm ambivalent on hunting, and so is Phil because we've both lived in the countryside. It's not a black and white argument. Most of the time, to a folk audience, you're speaking to the converted about issues: economic, civil liberties, women's rights, they already agree with you. But if you're in a village hall with a lot of farmers and country people who might not agree with you, you cannot tub-thump to that crowd, you have to tell them a story which maybe makes them think 'Yeah, that's true', they recognise a truth in it.."*

STEVE: *"Just because music is important to you it doesn't mean it has a right necessarily to be listened to. You have to see yourself in context all the time, and you have to see yourself in the big picture, not just because you may be a big name in your particular genre.."*
Stills from the photoshoot for
The Long Way Home

2010

✤ Show of Hands are awarded Best Live Act at The BBC Folk Awards success, and Arrogance Ignorance & Greed wins the Best Song award

✤ The bands PR machine, of Jane Brace, Bobbie Coppen and Amanda Beel are kept busy securing and managing various TV and media exposure in the wake of the Folk Awards successes

✤ 'Standing Room Only' Tour with Ruarri Joseph support

✤ The Spring 2010 Show of Hands newsletter declares that "our model of self reliance and close relationship with our audience is regarded as a role model of contemporary business marketing throughout the music industry"

✤ Phil undergoes minor heart surgery and proclaims that "news of my demise has been greatly exaggerated"!

✤ Spires and Beams Tour with Jackie Oates or Phillip Henry & Hannah Martin as support

✤ Autumn Tour with Rodney Branigan as support

✤ Covers 2 is released – another opportunity to showcase some of the bands favourite songs by other songwriters

✤ Phil's compilation Box Set One is finally released

Fairport's Cropredy Convention 20*

"We were an hour the wrong side of the Avo
when the old van gave up the fight

A LIFE ON STAGE AND ON THE ROA

SHOW OF HANDS 25TH

Top: Cropredy
Left: Off on tour, Topsham
Above: Assembly Halls, Tunbridge Wells,

Opposite, top: Afternoon set at the Cambridge Festival; with friend Steve Weaver and first wife Simone, animated audience and leaving the stage prior to an encore
Bottom of page: Steve prepares for a gig, Detail of 'Acoustic Pre-amp'
STEVE: *"...With John Godsland, a local technology boffin, we have created a phantom powered mic, stand-mounted, mutable DI (Direct Injection) box incorporating an acoustic guitar pre-amp volume, tone controls and auxiliary output, and so replacing up to four or five units. I've been using it now for the best part of twenty years."*
(Photos taken for the 2009 Track Of Words Retraced album packaging)

STEVE: *"Phil keeps what I do grounded in that sense, he's my connection to the folk scene and always was. Musically it's that ability to decorate what I create with so many different textures, and without putting his ego into it. He doesn't think of the solo as his big moment of the night, it's just another thing he plays. He's studiously neutral about all that, which is good because I can then waffle on and talk about this and that and Phil just stands there and the next minute he starts playing."*

"He doesn't feel the need to get profound, his only real foible on stage is he has an absolute love about talking about dead people."

PHIL: *"There's something quite grounded about what we do. We put on a great show, there's no question about that, I don't think there are many other groups of musicians in our genre that take that amount of trouble with their big show, it's well presented, so you get the feeling that you've just been to see a major band, even if you've just been to see a band that no-one else has heard of.*

We've always been ahead of the game regarding production technology. We can't divorce what we do from technology: if we're going to deliver to a big audience we need a state of the art PA and the best technicians. If people don't go away thinking they've been to something on the same level in terms of its presentation as say, Eric Clapton at the Albert Hall, we haven't done our job properly."

"And it's the standard of the show, we keep the standard of the recordings as good as we can make them within the budget, bearing in mind we have no record company, we make the records, we pay for all this. Everything is self-contained, which is in itself part of the ethos. I'm not going to say it's our magnetic personalities. I do think it's possible that we generate something; on a good night I think we can generate a chemistry. It can work extremely well, on a good night."

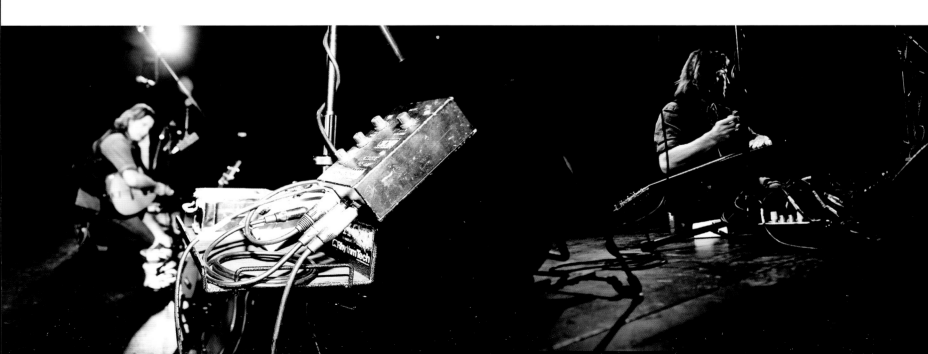

PHIL: *"I could see some of the key songs that people were responding to. People would come up to talk about the songs, so it was obvious that we were making some kind of impact upon people. The song called 'Man of War' that we were doing which was one of Steve's slightly trad-y sounding but modern songs which uses a lot of metaphor, there were obvious things — we'll never shake off 'The Galway Farmer', that is our 'Streets of London'. Great fun as well."*

STEVE: *"No person's occupation is nobler than any other person's. Everybody has something to contribute, everybody has a story."*

When compiling a set, a song impacts on those either side, both in terms of its musical and emotional delivery is taken into account in the way a director might approach a drama — to heighten the audience's experience. Show of Hands also see the demand for standards. But rather than play other people's songs Knightley composes his own. Understanding the mechanics of musical immediacy, he'll take a well-known rhythm and chord progression and make it theirs - his flair for melody and lyrics being matched by Beer's talent for improvisation and an ear for tunes that create sweet unexpected harmonies. From the start Show of Hands could deliver the comfort of the familiar with the excitement of the new, (that's at the heart of every 'instant classic') not just in the running-order of songs, but within the songs themselves.

Sidestepping rehearsals the pair would work out new songs during the sound check. "I drive a song along on guitar or mandolin and Phil plays all the decorative parts. He's got a choice of four instruments to decorate it. I've got four instruments to play on. So in that mathematical combination lies the possibilities for the arrangements." And getting to know their regular audiences they'd ask for their input during the gig. "This is a new one. We're working on it. What do you think?"

It's a way of working that's sustaining as it provides flexibility. Their relationship with the audience allows them to rework old songs, stripping them bare, changing the rhythm or the tempo, dusting them down, keeping them relevant, fresh with new life. "What do you think? Let us know." With The Dive, "for years it was in a very fixed rhythm with an amplified drum beat in the body of the cello mandolin which we manipulated in the PA to make it sound like a submarine's sonar. Now we've completely revamped it. It now has the feel of a claw-hammer, evenly pitched '60s folk song in the way Ralph McTell might do it." By including the audience in this process, Show of Hands are freed from the constraining demand to always hear an old-favourite in the same way.

Above, left to right: Labadoux Festival, Ingelmunster, Flanders, Belgium 2003, Cambridge afternoon set in 1997, Paul Downes soundchecking at Eden Project 2003 (flouting Knightley's no shorts on stage rule).
Right: Phil soundcheck at Eden, Steve in Holland.

PHIL: *"By now we were doing a lot of larger gigs, we were going abroad quite a bit still. There is a fixed number of largish folk-type festivals and you get booked to play them once every couple of years, or maybe once every 3 years. If you're comfortably playing in an arts centre that's selling out with 350-400 people, some of the biggest issues are to find the 500-600 seat theatres, they are the primary problem... You have a problem when you want to play Aylesbury, for instance, and you've got a choice between a 150-seater and a 1,400-seater. You've got no choice but to go to the 1,400 seater where maybe you'll be lucky and get about 800 in, but it looks half full. It's still brilliant because you're getting 800 people but it looks half full. It's a perpetual problem."*

STEVE: *"We both agree that what defines what you do is your life work, as much as anything. That's what you depend on, that's your currency. We both agree about always giving an audience its due worth, its respect."*

PHIL: *"You get asked: what kind of music do you play? So you say folk music, well that will immediately alienate 99% of the world. So you try not to say that, although that is the category that it gets firmly placed in. One of the inevitable conclusions that people jump to is that it's got something to do with country music. In any case, there are also various silly terminologies like acid, folk and new folk, which couldn't be further from what we do. So you have the problem of attempting to explain the thing that you do, even though once people hear it they immediately get it."*

STEVE: " 'To busy giddy minds with foreign travel.' In the early days with Gerard's encouragement we did a lot of tours to exotic locations: India, Malaysia, Hong Kong, Spain and Australia. We had an extraordinary time, and the experience informed the music but it never opened up any subsequent concert touring opportunity. I wouldn't have missed it for the world... When Vaughan and Gwen took over the reins we concentrated much more on England... after all, there's a lot of us in a tiny country!"

Show of Hands visit India (1997), Australia (1998), Indonesia and Spain (1996)

STEVE: *"Miranda roots the music, she gives it shape. If there's a bass note out with our chords it can sound awful. When you say to her, do you know the chords, she won't say 'yeah,' in a kind of blokey, 'It'll be alright' manner she wants to know exactly how they go. And she drives us into structure, a lot more than if we were just a duo. Some of the best musicians I know are women because they don't wing it."*

When Miranda Sykes joined the band in 2004, Show of Hands were playing to audiences of about 100 to 150 people. Now the regular size is about 600. And not only has the audience grown but their way of working changed when she came on board.

Show of Hands are unashamedly professional in their approach. And it's from this professionalism that the easy two-way inter-connection with their audience springs. With their well-honed stagecraft there is no disconnect between them and their audience. When Knightley announced from the stage that his son Jack had been given the all-clear from Leukaemia (fans had raised money for his treatment and Nettlebed folk club had a tree-house built for him), there appeared to be no difference between the performer and the thankful private man. They deliver authenticity. And this authenticity connects with audiences across the world as the band finds language is no barrier to building their cross-cultural community.

Opposite, top to bottom:
Miranda at Cardiff December 2008,
Phil at Cropredy 2004, Steve at the Floral
Pavilion New Brighton, The Wirral 2012,
Main picture:
Miranda at the Half Moon, Putney 2007 and
(inset) on the Autumn tour, 2004.
Above: Village Pump Festival, Trowbridge 2015,
Above: Backstage at Yeovil 2008
Left: At the Beautiful Days Festival, Devon 2007

STEVE: *"Canada has some of the finest folk festivals on the scene, and we were lucky enough to have met Leonard Podolak playing with the Duhks in Canmore in 2005. We have since toured with Lenny and he was also involved in the Cecil Sharp project. We'd love to go back and play there again sometime."*

STEVE: "*Phil and I were lucky enough to be asked to be patrons of the Village Pump, Sidmouth and St Ives festivals. The festival circuit is thriving in England from May to September.*"
Main picture: Miranda, at The Village Pump Festival Trowbridge 2006
Top to bottom: Phil on stage at the Larmer Tree Festival 2007, Phil and Steve at the Cropredy Festival 2000, Steve at Abbotsbury

MIRANDA: "*I can't imagine working with anyone else like I work with Show of Hands, it just feels right really. I don't know what I brought to it. People keep telling me that it's brilliant and that it's changed with me but I don't know. I can only believe what people say really which is that the band is immense and that it's such a great sound with the three harmonies and the double bass. It feels right...*"

Show of Hands strengthen their audience's sense of community by inviting them to take part in the show as quickly as possible. As everyone joins in the singing there's a palpable sense of joyous inclusion that lasts beyond the end of each performance. They also extend that idea of belonging to the support acts that accompany them. Learning from Ralph McTell who knew that audiences had pitched up to see him and would only want to see an act that he particularly liked, Show of Hands are careful in their choice of support artists. They look for people who can connect with the audience, who interact with the crowd rather than spending the night gazing at their shoes and mumbling. They have helped the careers of several young musicians, including Kate Rusby, Seth Lakeman, Luke Jackson, Philip Henry and Hannah Martin.

By introducing their support every night, Show of Hands enfold those musicians into their community, directing towards them that current of connection with their audience. In this way (as well as through extensive production work) they have helped the careers of several young musicians. Knightley says: "Phil mentored and produced Jackie Oates and I also discovered this young girl Jenna Witts and produced her first two albums. Kate Rusby's first major tour as a solo artist was on our "Five Days in May" tour of 5 major venues across the country in 1997. Phil Henry and Hannah Martin I found busking on Sidmouth seafront and we gave them their first touring opportunity. Seth Lakeman's first solo touring opportunity was with Western Approaches, a tour with me and Jenna in 2014. We've also toured and been involved with Jim Causely and The India Electric Company who are all local lads".

The community feeling is also underlined by the regular guest appearances of many musician friends like Paul Downes, Matt Clifford, Tom Robinson and Martyn Joseph, at Show of Hands gigs, adding to the surprise of the night. For Show of Hands offering both a comforting and exciting new experience is key to their live performances - wherever the gig might be.

STEVE: "I'm probably the only person to ever have worn an Exeter Chiefs Rugby shirt at the Royal Albert Hall"
Above left: Phil at Cropredy 2000
Above right: Steve backstage at the Royal Albert Hall 7th April 2012
Below: Cropredy Village Hall run by 'Aunt' Shirley Kershaw 12th July 2007
Tuning up at the Northcott Theatre Exeter 2003

2011

✤ Steve publishes Songbook 3

✤ Backlog Tour featuring songs from the first 10 years, with Longdogs voting for a Top 20 which will form the track list of the Backlog 2 album

✤ Autumn tour with Richard Shindell as support

✤ Show of Hands have established themselves as a theatre act, occasionally playing arts centres, and playing smaller venues for fun and to maintain contact with the folk club circuit that supported them in the early years

✤ Steve is asked to be Patron of Shrewsbury Festival

SHOW of HANDS
with MIRANDA SYKES

shrewsbury FOLK festival

AND MIRANDA SYKES REX PRESTON

SHOW of HANDS
The New Album
COVERS 2
Available from
www.showofhands.co.uk or at

JANUARY 2011		
	RUGBY ROOTS, LAWRENCE SHERIFF SCHOOL	01788 567338
THU 27	QUEENS PARK CENTRE, AYLESBURY	01296 424 332
FRI 28	QUEEN ELIZABETH HOSPITAL, BRISTOL	0117 99299008
SAT 29	HAMBLEDON VILLAGE HALL, HANTS	023 92 632418
SUN 30		

FEBRUARY 2011		
	THE CELLARS AT EASTNEY	023 92826249
WED 2	BRIDPORT ARTS CENTRE, BRIDORT	01308 424204
THU 3	FARNCOMBE MUSIC CLUB, FARNCOMBE	01483 421520
FRI 4	BOURNEMOUTH FOLK CLUB, BOURNEMOUTH	01202 707498
SAT 5	HITCHIN FOLK CLUB, HITCHIN	01462 812391
SUN 6	NETTLEBED VILLAGE CLUB	01628 636620
WED 9	THE PRINCE ALBERT, STROUD	01453 755600
THU 10	NATIONAL CENTRE FOR EARLY MUSIC, YORK	01904 658338
FRI 11	FARNFIELD ACOUSTIC, NOTTINGHAMSHIRE	01623 870668
SAT 12	NEW CUT HALESWORTH, SUFFOLK	0845 6732123
SUN 13	THE GUILDHALL, LEICESTER	0116 253 269
WED 16	HUNGRY HORSE FOLK CLUB, WIRRAL	0151 6789902
THU 17	BURNLEY MECHANICS, BURNLEY	01282 664400
FRI 18	SALE FOLK CLUB, SALE, MANCHESTER	0161 4324317
SAT 19	ACOUSTIC TEA ROOMS	01768 372123
SUN 20	KIRBY STEPHENS, LAKE DISTRICT	01395 227887
WED 23	BLACKMORE THEATRE, EXMOUTH	01905 611427
THU 24	HUNTINGDON HALL, WORCESTER	01902 57228
FRI 25	NEWHAMPTON ARTS CENTRE	
	NEWHAMPTON, NR WOLVERHAMPTON	01458 44284
SAT 26	STRODE THEATRE, STREET	01392 66700
SUN 27	PHOENIX EXETER	

SOLO TOUR 2011

www.showofhands.co.uk
www.myspace.com/steveknightleymusic / www.myspace.com/jimcausle

SHOW of HANDS Backlog 2

STEVE KNIGHTLEY

PHIL: *"Playing live is great, it's simply the grind of getting there, it's nothing to do with the actual performance. If you could be beamed there then that would be lovely, but I think a lot of people feel like that about life in general."*

STEVE: *"I think what kick-started it was just the need to connect to people and how nice it felt when people applauded. But one thing I always knew, and I still know this to this day, is that if you have a need to be applauded there's never enough, whether it's a family or a room full or a small club, or the Albert Hall, it is, by its nature, never sufficient; you always want another fix of it... Also, and this surprises people because they always ask you what your favourite gig is, to play to a village hall of 90 people on that day is as nourishing as to play to the Albert Hall full of 5,000. It's not bigger because there's more of it. It doesn't feel like that any more than a meal at a 5-star restaurant is better than a wonderful barbecue by the sea two days later: because you need a meal, you need food, you need contact. When I look at putting a show together I don't think of what can I do next, I sit in the audience and think "What would be a good thing to happen now, after that last bit?". I sit there and think "OK, that was the sound, that was the texture, that was that. Wouldn't it be great if they did something unaccompanied, wouldn't it be good if Miranda did that". Then I work backwards and fit the material into the cadence of the shape that I make. And it usually works ".*

"I'm always thinking of the needs of the show. I'm always thinking 'OK we need some up-tempo songs, we need some singalong songs, we need a bit of darkness, we need Phil to play an instrumental... You just have to keep the standard up. And that's one thing where Phil is probably more conscientious than me, he will not relax his standards on sound and production. My attitude sometimes is "Oh we can get by, at the end of the day they'll clap and they'll love it". But Phil, believes this: that you're only as good as your last gig. I know it's a cliché but for Phil that is axiomatic, that's one of the principles by which he operates.

Extraordinarily, of the thousands and thousands and thousands of gigs that we've done, even in terms of transport chaos or last minute disasters or whatever may befall us, he's never not done the show. He's never not delivered what he delivers. And I don't know where we get those standards from really, because there's a part of us which is quite – not lazy, but we don't rehearse a lot – but we've never let down an audience I don't think."

"*Maybe once when I was drinking with 'The Levellers' at a festival in Germany all day have I let down a crowd. I thought I could go head-to-head with Mark, hang out with the guys all day and still deliver a coherent festival show, but I lost all my instincts.*"

"*There's a part of us which is very fit and very good at this, and we do not have nights off, we never do. I see other bands have nights off all the time, they'll talk about 'Oh that wasn't a good audience' and they accept maybe one gig in three not clicking. But we just never do that, and I think people realise that, and I don't quite know how we've done it sometimes but even with bereavement in the family, even when my son was ill we still go out and do the gig...*

...I thought the need to be applauded was somehow a weakness or a frailty. And I remember when I first met Clare, 'There's one thing you need to know about me, I've got this need to be clapped' blah blah blah, and she said 'I just thought it was your job'. And that was the single most inspiring thing. 'It's just your job isn't it? I'm a doctor, why do I want to get into the point of motivation? Just do your job, what's the big deal?' And then it was a job, like my dad had a job, it's what men do to raise their kids, it's a job. And that's what I say to these younger musicians, 'don't beat yourself up about it, just do it'. What redeems it is how well you do it and the relationships you build."

All pictures: Cropredy 2004 except top right.
Miranda at the Waterfont Norwich 2011

STEVE: *"We leave each other alone. We can drive to London and not say a word, literally, there's no pauses that anyone feels a need to fill. I think we know each other's strengths and weaknesses. As I say, Phil's got no agenda, he's never in my face saying 'Oh what about that, when are we going to do that; I'd like to sing that song'. He usually lets the business tick over with occasionally one or two rather brutal interventions. On the whole he lets me steer it along."*

2012

❖ Steve touring with Phil & Hannah and Cecil Sharp Project

❖ Another Royal Albert Hall gig to celebrate 20 years of solid touring

❖ This years Abbotsbury is abandoned due to torrential rain...

❖ Wake The Union is released – a rich array of guest artists include: Martin Simpson, Seth Lakeman, BJ Cole, Andy Cutting, Paul Sartin, Cormac Byrne, Paul Downes, Phil Henry, Hannah Martin, Rex Preston and Jenna

❖ Producer Mark Tucker multi-tasks and films much of the recording process – the resulting film will be edited as "Making The Waking"

❖ Two songs from the album came out of songwriting workshop events at Dartington and Herstmonceux Castle

❖ A (low budget!) video is produced for the single Company Town

❖ 'Wake The Union' Autumn Tour in support of the album of the same name

❖ Support is by Matt Gordon & Leonard Podolak

❖ SOH host a two day residential session at Portmeirion

❖ The Shrewsbury Festival set is a special affair featuring the Urban Soul Orchestra

SHOW of HANDS

Wake the Union

AUNT MARIA 2.43   KING OF THE WORLD 2.34

SHOW OF HANDS
COMPANY TOWN

Set One
1) The Galway Farmer - Duo

2) The Blind Fiddler - Duo
   (Matt on)

3) Exile - Duo + Piano
   (Matt off. Miranda on)

4) Tall ships - Trio

5) You're mine - Trio

6) The Keys of Canterbury - Trio
   (Richard on)

7) You Stay Here - Trio + RS
   (Phil/Miranda off. Phil H/Hannah on)

8) Reunion Hill - SK/PH/HM/RS
   (Phil/Miranda on. Richard/Hannah off)

9) Country life - Trio + PH

Set Two
1) Innocents song - Trio + Strings

2) Are we Alright - Trio + Strings
   (Matt on)

3) The Dive - Trio + Strings + Piano
   (Matt off)

4) Cuthroats - Trio

5) AIG - Trio
   (Matt on)

6) Cousin Jack - Trio + Piano
   (Raffle Draw)

7) IED - Trio + Strings + Piano

8) Cockade - Trio + Strings + Piano
   (Matt off)

9) Roots - Trio

10) Now you know - Trio
    Encore
    (All on)
    Santiago - Trio + The Company

SHOW OF HANDS
COMPANY TOWN – NOW YOU KNOW

STEVE: " I don't regard what I do as being particularly important. I don't regard it as art. I look at what we do as a craft…"

"…I would much rather see myself in the tradition of a storyteller than an artist…"

" …Most people I know who wish to talk about their artistic temperament are often justifying bad behaviour by being late and having no manners, I don't buy into that…"

" …I think you can look back at the career of a musician like Bob Dylan or Martin Carthy and when you consider a lifetimes work, you can say 'That was an artist'. "

Abbotsbury Festival, which Show of Hands
put on for the first time in 1998. Featuring
themselves and sets by special guests, they
welcome the audience to spend the day
with them at what feels like a private garden
party. This sense of inclusion is integral
to Show of Hands as they provide a real,
appealing sense of community with their
music at its heart.

RUNNING ORDER

5·30 – 6·15: SOH
(INC ALL OF TALL SHIPS)
SETUP
6·30 – 7·00 VLADIMIR VEGA
7·15 – 8·00 ENGLISH MUSIC
WITH PHIL BEER
& GARETH TURNER !!!
8·15 – 8·45 SIX NEW MEXICODIA
SONGS WITH
STEVE KNIGHTLEY
9·00 – 10·00 – SOH !

Right: Steve and Phil with Port Isaac's
Fisherman's Friends in Port Isaac 2001
Above: West Country's finest - Bill Hawkins
with Steve and Seth Lakeman
Bottom: Oysterband 'Big Session' advert
featuring Show of Hands.
Bottom, left to right.
Phil looking out aboard The Tectona,
Steve playing onboard
The Pegasus in Dartmouth

One secret to the success of Show of Hands longer-than-most-marriages relationship is that Knightley, Beer and Sykes, all actively pursue their own musical interests outside the band. This brings them recognition and acclaim beyond their identity as a duo/trio.

It's no secret that throughout Show of Hands career Phil Beer has maintained an extraordinary gigging and recording schedule both as a solo artist - in duos with Paul Downes, Johnny Coppin and Deb Sandland as well as with his own Phil Beer Band. Not including his work with the Albion Band, Beer has released 23 albums to date with a huge new retrospective album project in the pipeline.

Beer was able to combine his love of sailing and of tall ships when he helped crew The Pegasus in the annual Tall Ships race in 2009, to finish 2nd. despite having to stop for repairs in St. Petersburg. The nine-week race over 4,500 nautical miles took in twelve countries and in taking part Beer realised a cherished dream.

Beer combines his love of music with sailing on his "folk boat" project, popular events where sailing is combined with on board music workshops and impromptu performances. Whilst together with Knightley the duo sailed down the Rhine and perform on board as Show of Hands.

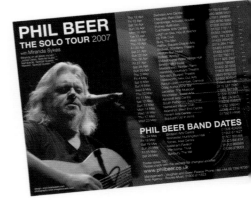

Above: Phil Beer solo tour flyer
Above, left: The Pegasus in St Petersburg
Below: Phil Beer Band at Morchard Bishop
Devon 2001,
Phil giving a house concert in 2007 with
Emily Sanders formerly of Isambarde
Bottom and Right: Phil on the Folk Boat

Above: Steve with Seth Lakeman
and Jenna Witts
Right and Below: Steve, Tom Robinson and
Martyn Joseph - Faith, Folk and Anarchy
Bottom, left to right: Steve solo tour publicity
with Jim Causley supporting, a backstage chat
with Afrocelts Johnny Kalsi which lead to the
co-write of the Dohl Foundations 'Mother
Tongue' single. Steve's 'All At Sea' press shot,
Two more gigs with Martyn Joseph.

Knightley's love of the sea is clear in his latest solo tour and album 2016's "All At Sea" with gigs around the shoreline of England and Wales. This follows hot on the heals of his extensive 160 "Grow Your Own Gig" tour which saw him perform at village halls across the country. Knightley has released nine albums either as a solo artist or in collaborations with artists both young and old - including as a trio – Faith Folk and Anarchy with Tom Robinson and Martyn Joseph – and with Seth Lakeman and Jenna Witts, and again in a duo with Joseph.

Knightley also produced Jez Lowe's Jack Common's Anthem and separately and together, both Beer and Knightley help promote the careers of a new generation of artists, whether through producing their albums or inviting them on tour or both, Beer notably working with Jackie Oates and Tom Palmer and Knightley with Hannah and Phil, Jenna and Seth Lakeman.

Above: Phil – always a keen photographer

Above, left: The inner-sanctum at The Bridge Inn, Topsham, Phil's local with a gang of friends including Dave Lowry, Barry Lister, Jackie Oates and Jim Causley

Top left: Phil has always kept a close connection to the local Exeter traditional folk scene. Some of the singers that he first met back at The Jolly Porter still perform at The Topsham Folk Club

Middle left: Phil photographed at Abbotsbury 2016 by super-fan Nick Pilley

Below left: Phil is thrilled that his sister's kids have taken up the baton and are playing traditional folk music.

Below: Phil meets up with Paul Downes, backstage at Abbotsbury... still crazy after all these years.

STEVE: "*Phil has no interest in sport whatsoever, apart from yachting and I'm not sure that really counts. When Show of Hands started performing, Exeter Chiefs were playing in the lower reaches of English rugby in a funny sort of way our ascent up the English folk ladder has matched their rise to becoming one of Europes top sides. And it's great to see the same old faces at Sandy Park that I saw when I was a kid living next to the old County Ground.*"

"*I've still got some friends from John Stocker School. Andy Worth at the Exeter Rugby Club, one of their team managers, I still see him regularly. And living next to the old County ground I fell in love with the Exeter Rugby Team at that point as well, and speedway on a Monday night. As a kid, in order to develop strategies to make friends it was either sport or entertainment – or fooling about. What got you a pat on the head was sport or entertainment....*

...A dream day for me would probably be to go and see Exeter Chiefs in the afternoon, win, preferably against Wasps, to drive down to a little village hall, say Modbury, playing to 150 people, to have a drink with some friends after the gig. In other words basically next Saturday. What a nice day."

Opposite:
Twickenham 2016 - The Aviva
Championship Final versus Saracens

"On the day after the Cropredy Festival there is always a cricket match between the musicians and the villagers. In the team that day you might recognise Richard Thompson, Danny Thompson, Simon Nichol and Dave Pegg - along with Gerard O'Farrell and my old mate Steve Sheldon...

I'm too modest to point out that, on this particular day I was man of the match."

2013

✤ A busy Summer again – Including outings at the Royal Festival Hall, Beverley Folk Festival, Sidmouth, Towersey, the annual Unison conference in Liverpool and a benefit show at the local retail outlet Darts Farm in aid of the Devon Air Ambulance

✤ The Shrewsbury Folk Festival gig is released on DVD alongside Making The Waking. The Shrewsbury performance is a unique collaboration with the Urban Soul Orchestra

✤ Steve finally embarks on his 'Grow Your Own Gig' Tour – an initiative to turn fans into promoters by encouraging them to host their own Knightley concert in village halls and community centres

✤ A 10-date German tour is followed up by a 29-date jaunt around the UK – The Hand in Hand Tour

STEVE: *"It was odd doing a session with Mick Jagger, sitting opposite him round a microphone because part of you thinks that's one of the most famous people in the world, and part of you thinks it's just this skinny old cockney..."*

...When I met Peter Gabriel, who I've always idolised, he said some very kind things about my writing. It took me a while to take on board what he was saying, but I wasn't star-struck I was just appreciative...
...We did a show at the Eden Project. We didn't expect him and his whole band to watch us play from the side all night, we thought they'd just turn up. He came up and said 'You have written many fine songs', and I said 'Yeah, it was a good gig'. He said 'No, listen, you've written many fine songs', and I said 'Yeah, thank you'. It was almost like 'Listen, I'm saying something to you, don't just waffle on, just listen to what I'm saying'. I took that on board. He was trying to say something and I was just saying 'Oh, it's just a good gig wasn't it'. So that was very nice...

I'd like to do more with Peter Gabriel, but I'd love it if Bruce Springsteen stood at the back of one of our gigs and said 'Yeah, I recognise this stuff, this is real'. That would be great...

...Anthony Martin comes to a lot of our gigs and it'd be great to meet his son Chris. I like the fact that Coldplay are still committed to melodic rock songs, they don't feel the need to reinvent themselves and become ironic and post-modern. They want people to stand in a field and sing along and have a communal experience. So I'd rather take issue with those that attack them for that, because they don't let down the audience. As a local lad, the way he connected with the audience at the Powderham Castle gig was fantastic...
...My sister asked Anthony if Chris would dedicate 'Fix You' to my late brother's nephew, Robbie, at their Etihad Stadium show. The fact that the request got through and the dedication was made implies a level of compassion that transcends all of the froth and fame that comes with 'stardom'. It would be nice to sit in a back room of a Devon pub and strum a few songs with him sometime. "

2014

❖ A year of mainly solo activity
Phil organises 'Folk Boat' – musical
sailing workshops

❖ Steve running Abbotsbury with friends – Including
Miranda Sykes & Rex Preston; Sheelanagig, Phil
Henry & Hannah Martin; Steve Knightley & Friends
and the ridiculously young & talented siblings
Aimeé, Freya and Ross Mackenzie

❖ Steve hosts another workshop event at
Herstmonceux Castle, with a one-off concert
featuring the "Wake the Union" band; Martin
Simpson, recognised as one of the best guitar
players in the world and melodeon maestro Andy
Cutting, Miranda Sykes and Rex Preston and newly
crowned Best Duo at the 2014 BBC Radio 2 Folk
Awards – Phillip Henry and Hannah Martin

❖ Saturday 20th September SOH appear as part
of the Candlelit Concert series in the new Sam
Wanamaker Playhouse at Shakespeare's
Globe in London

❖ Show of Hands appear with Jim Carter on the
Andrew Marr Remembrance Day TV Show, Steve and
Jim also do interviews on Breakfast TV
Steve Knightley 'Grow Your Own Gig'
Tour continues

❖ Costa Del Folk – Show of Hands are booked for a
Folk 'getaway' in sunny Portugal

❖ Autumn Tour – After an eight month break, Steve,
Phil and Miranda are back on the road together for
the SOH Autumn Tour, kicking off at Ipswich Corn
Exchange and culminating in two nights at
Exmouth Pavilion

❖ The Release of 'Centenary' on the 100th
anniversary of the start of the Great War – a concept
album based on the poetry and music of the War. A
project born following discusssions between Steve
Knightley and songwriter/music business friend and
entrepreneur Ian Brown. The album is released and
given a TV advertised release through Universal
Music, and among other media exposure is featured
on the Mark Radcliffe Show in July 2014

STEVE: "It's always great to share a stage with mates. I know some artists who don't even know who's playing whilst they're waiting in the dressing room to headline. We like to think of ourselves as a family, then the whole evening has a sort of unity about it."

Among the artists that have shared a stage with Show of Hands are:
Left to right, top to bottom: Miranda and Rex, Martin Simpson, Seth Lakeman, Jackie Oates, Megan Henwood, Sunjay, Slaid Cleaves, Rodney Branigan, Martyn Joseph (seen here duetting with Miranda), Athene Roberts of Three Daft Monkeys, Jenna Witts, India Electric Company, Luke Jackson, Flossie Malavialle, Philip and Hannah, Phil Beer with Deb Sandland and Leonard Podolak and Matt Gordon.

STEVE *"I think most artists make too many records. They make a record a year, it's too much. You should let the stuff go out there and percolate around a bit more than most people do. So I think we'll probably make a record every two years. Just keep looking for those other themes, like 'Centenary', those other ideas, other collaborations, keep encouraging and working with the younger generation which is what we both enjoy doing anyway."*

Centenary (2014), a series of instrumental settings of WW1 poetry and original commemorative songs by Show of Hands featuring popular instrumentation of the time appealed to fans and new crowds alike. This also produced a live CD recorded in Exeter Cathedral where the poems were read by Knightley's old mate Jim Carter (who had collaborated with Knightley on Tall Ships in the late '80s.) and his wife Imelda Staunton.

On this project Knightley's flair for narrative brings history smack bang wallop to bloody visceral life. With his ability to lob issues that affect people in a particular place and time into the hearts and minds of people far removed from it, he makes those issues relevant and meaningful to everyman. He focuses our attention so the strings of our interconnection through time and geographical space resonate with our awareness. And Beer and Sykes powerfully reinforce this with musical motifs that echo with collective memory. Knightley further strengthens this sense of connection through songs that compel people to sing along - and so confirm their place in a community in a particular moment in the continuum of time. And this after all, is what folk music is supposed to do.

Top, left to right: '19240 – Shrouds of the Somme' Exeter July 2016, Imelda Staunton and Jim Carter performing with Show of Hands at Exeter Cathedral.
Above: Sergeant Thomas James Knightley of the Dorset Regiment (circa 1911)
Opening ceremony of '19240 Shrouds of the Somme' which commemorated the lives of those lost on the first day of the battle of the Somme. Seen far left, the artist Rob Heard, who created the art installation of 19,240 twelve inch figures, each one wrapped and bound in a hand-stitched shroud and arranged in rows on the ground outside Exeter Castle.
Right: Miranda, Phil, Andrew Marr, Jim Carter and Steve after an appearance on the Andrew Marr Show, Alternate cover proposals for the album

2015

✤ No spring tour, both Steve and Phil committed to solo tours for start of year

✤ Steve's never ending tour of village halls - 'Grow Your Own Gig' culminates in a big show at the prestigious St Georges Hall in Bristol whilst Phil Beer touring both solo and with the Phil Beer Band

✤ With Miranda's commitments to her duo collaboration with mandolin player Rex Preston, Steve and Phil produce a duo album. "The Long Way Home" is conceived as a back-to-basics folk album for the 21st century. They tour the album around the UK

✤ Miranda and Rex take Grant Gordy on tour as their special guest

✤ Phil undertakes a new series of Folk Boat music and sailing trips.

✤ 23 September: Steve, Phil and Miranda are presented with Honorary Doctorates of Music from Plymouth University

✤ Miranda and Dan get married

✤ October: Return to Costa Del Folk, Portugal together with Seth Lakeman, Barbara Dickson, Coco and the Butterfields, Demon Barbers, and Mike Harding

✤ The Long Way Home secures healthy radio airplay with tracks featured on Bob Harris, Tom Robinson and Mark Radcliffe's shows

"We might be a little older now but the heart beat is still as strong"

PAYING IT FORWARD AND THE ROAD AHEAD

2016

❖ Year starts with Walk with Me making Radio 2 playlists, and Show of Hands 'In Session' with Mark Radcliffe

❖ Rhine River Cruise

❖ Spring 'Long Way Home' Tour (Duo)

❖ Autumn Tour with support by Megan Henwood

❖ Friday 1st July: 19240 – Shrouds of the Somme; Show of Hands with special guests 'The Lost Sound Chorus' in concert at Exeter Cathedral.
This was a special World War 1 Centenary concert to commemorate the 19,240 Allied servicemen who lost their lives on the first day of the Battle of the Somme. Jim Carter and Imelda Staunton were special guests for this profoundly moving and memorable gig. The evening was recorded and released as Centenary Live at Exeter Cathedral in late 2016

❖ Release of 'Centenary Live'

❖ After 20 years working with SOH Vaughan & Gwen Pearce retire and hand over the business to Vicky Whitlock

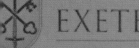

EXETER CATHEDRAL

U12

BOOKING REF: 20003959939

NAME: Steve Sheldon

EVENT: 19240 Shrouds of the Somme: Show of Hands

VENUE: Exeter Cathedral Seated

DATE & TIME: Friday, 01 July 2016 19:40

TICKET TYPE: Adult

PRICE: £21.00

The collaboration with Chilean musicians was to have a profound impact on Knightley's understanding of the sociopolitical implications of the power of music. It focused his attention on the reason for writing, "to inform, educate and entertain," insights which he passes on to fellow musicians in songwriting workshops such as at Dartington and Herstmonceux and at Beaminster Comprehensive, (where Knightley used to teach) which he ran with Billy Bragg and Simon Emmerson

Also shown left; a folder created by pupils of the Green Lane Community Special School in Warrington following their trip to see the band at the Lowry, Salford

As Show of Hands widen their audience, by 'word of mouth' on the internet and gig-by-gig-by-gig in real life, they increase that sense of community. Managed now by Vicky Whitlock who stepped up to the plate when Vaughan and Gwen Pearce retired, she first saw Show of Hands with her dad before leaving for university. Having subsequently steered both Beer and Knightley's solo careers she's best placed to guide their latest album and tour. Treading The Long Road Home, Show of Hands are bringing bigger broader audiences back to their folk roots from which it all began.

STEVE: *"A lot of what musicians say about how life on the road is tiring is a myth. It's exhausting if you stay up too late and drink too much, if you don't look after yourself, if you agree to stupid journeys which are ultimately your choice. You don't have to do that sort of thing. Generally speaking we're in a position now where the physically demanding side of it is minimal, we just have to stand and play for two hours, everybody claps you and tells you how great you are and gives you some money. What could be nicer?"*

PHIL:
*"He's slightly younger than me,
minutely younger than me.
He's several weeks
younger than me."*

STEVE:
"Eleven months actually."

STEVE: *"On our scene there are less headliners and we're still doing new stuff. It would be nice if we left a legacy of songs, it would be great if people can go and do pub gigs and sing one of my songs and people recognise it. To have increased the repertoire of the English would be a real legacy...*

...It's now accepted in the folk scene that we are the template by which you can make a career, and we should probably enjoy that status a bit more than we do. But we've still got a lot more to do."

"The current plan is to create a digital village that people can join in with. that would have access to so much material, and so much back-catalogue. We have a wonderful group of followers called 'The Long Dogs'; Facebook has supplanted their original website now. On their site they shared ticket dates, information, transport plans, they spoke about what they liked, what they didn't like, they reviewed our records. They started, if you like, as a Fan Club. It would be great to build on that community, by inventing a new model for it."

As well as providing songwriting workshops separately and as Show of Hands, both Beer and Knightley pay forward their vast experience in stagecraft and the business of music to the new generation of artists offering practical advice and support. As Ralph McTell once helped them so they now help others.

This extends to their tireless charity work, again either as solo artists or as Show of Hands. They have helped raise money for a variety of causes, both for specific communities such as saving the local post office and those that address global issues including autism, disadvantaged children and refugees.
Having started out on the Sidmouth folk circuit as young teenagers Show of Hands are now patrons of Sidmouth Folk Week as well as of the St Ives Festival. Knightley is also patron of the Shrewsbury Folk Festival and together they are patrons of Exeter's Royal Albert Memorial Museum & Art Gallery.

Paying it forward.
Giving back to the community that they continue to grow, Show of Hands keep on keeping on.

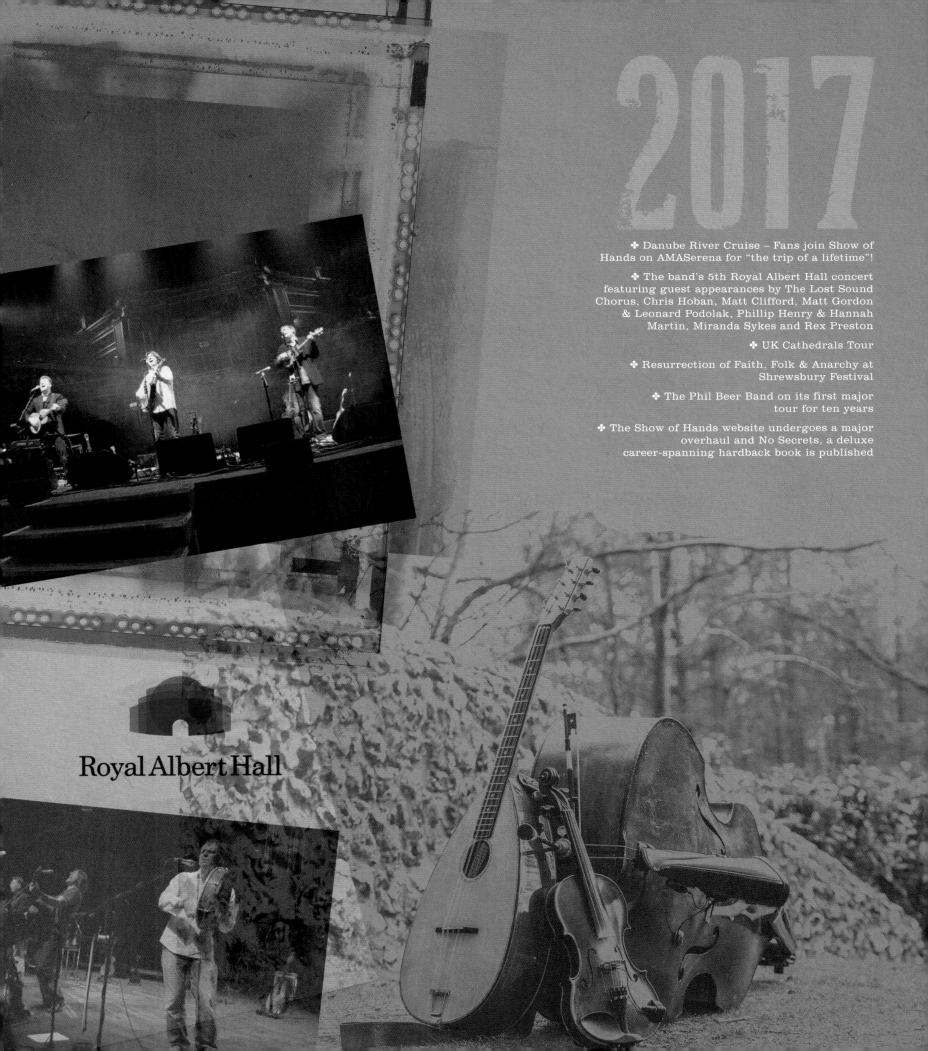

2017

✤ Danube River Cruise – Fans join Show of Hands on AMASerena for "the trip of a lifetime"!

✤ The band's 5th Royal Albert Hall concert featuring guest appearances by The Lost Sound Chorus, Chris Hoban, Matt Clifford, Matt Gordon & Leonard Podolak, Phillip Henry & Hannah Martin, Miranda Sykes and Rex Preston

✤ UK Cathedrals Tour

✤ Resurrection of Faith, Folk & Anarchy at Shrewsbury Festival

✤ The Phil Beer Band on its first major tour for ten years

✤ The Show of Hands website undergoes a major overhaul and No Secrets, a deluxe career-spanning hardback book is published

Royal Albert Hall

PHIL:
'Show of Hands' is a sense of history,
a sense of place, a sense of story.

STEVE: *"Show of Hands will go on 'til we drop. It's like jazz and blues – you do gain an extra level of credibility if you can age with dignity. You have to get through your 40s with a degree of dignity and not wear tight clothes or dye your hair. You can become cool again, like Eric Clapton and Willie Nelson. The folk scene's very good like that, there's no shelf life on it, no-one's going anywhere."*

PHIL.: *"It's a mutual fan club, there's absolutely no question about it. I greatly admire his songwriting skills, he greatly admires my multi-instrumental skills and together we are a formidable, earth-shattering, world-conquering, brand. You can quote me on that !"*

THE ALBUMS

SHOW OF HANDS *LIVE*
Phil Beer and Steve Knightley

SHOW OF HANDS
.B.E.A.T.

FOLK MUSIC

SHOW OF HANDS

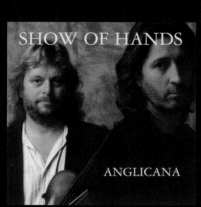

SHOW OF HANDS
ANGLICANA

SHOW OF HANDS
The Path

An instrumental journey around the West Country coastline

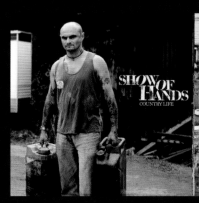

SHOW OF HANDS
COUNTRY LIFE

SHOW OF HANDS
as you were
LIVE ON TOUR AUTUMN 2004

SHOW of HANDS Backlog 2

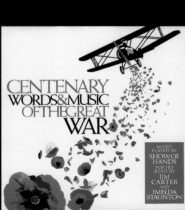

CENTENARY
WORDS & MUSIC OF THE GREAT WAR

MUSIC PLAYED BY SHOW OF HANDS
POETRY READ BY JIM CARTER AND IMELDA STAUNTON

TheLongWayHome
SHOW of HANDS

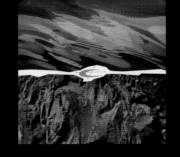

THE SONGBOOKS

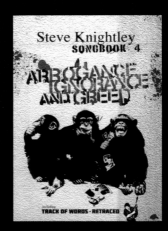
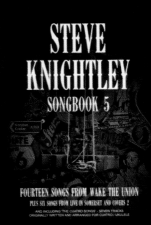

DVDS

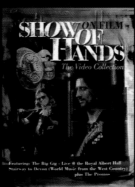

Richard Barnes:

"Longdogs" (or Show of Hands - Their part in my downfall)

It's 1996, the "child rearing years" are coming to a close, and our first visit to the Cropredy festival is eagerly anticipated.

I'd been particularly impressed by an article in Rock'n'Reel about one of the Cropredy acts, Show of Hands, and their Royal Albert Hall gig earlier that year. This was a duo I really wanted to see, and to say I wasn't disappointed is a huge understatement. The interaction between Steve and Phil was most impressive, Knightley's songs were superbly crafted and executed, the musicianship and vocal harmonies were first class, and unlike some of the earlier acts, they reached out to the top of the field and drew in the whole crowd. This was a class act. I headed straight to the merch tent after the set and bought a copy of every Show of Hands album they had, including "Show of Hands - Live at The Royal Albert Hall - 24th March 1996" which was to occupy my CD player on repeat play for several weeks.

Later I had the pleasure of meeting Steve & Phil, along with manager and sound guy Gerard O'Farrell and merch man Vaughan Pearce. Many more gigs followed, and in parallel we'd got on-line and were connecting with many fellow Fairport fans via their internet mailing list. It was a terrific resource and a great way of meeting like minded people. Show of Hands would often be mentioned on the FC list, there was clearly a lot of interest out there, maybe it was time that SoH had their own internet mailing list.

I had a number of discussions with Gerard about possibly setting up an internet mailing list – Gerard would go along with it if Steve and Phil were in agreement."The Supernet" took off. My partner in crime Alex Mowbray got on board early on to look after all the techie stuff, he came up with the name "Longdogs" and masterminded the development of the mailing list format and the eventual move to a web based forum.

Longdogs worked alongside Show of Hands in many great projects, notably exclusive charity CD releases, special gigs, and block bookings for big gigs such as subsequent Royal Albert Hall shows.

In parallel with the rise of Longdogs we did indeed start promoting gigs in and around Rugby. Inevitably Show of Hands, Steve solo, Phil solo and SoH related performers such as Miranda, Seth Lakeman, Jenna, Kathryn and Sean, etc etc featured heavily in our programmes over the years.

Sadly we've had to rein back on Longdogs recently due to other commitments, but happily Longdogs still exists in the form of a Facebook group and SoH's activities remain a big part of our lives, as it has for the last 21 years. So thanks for the ride Steve, Phil and the "gang". I congratulate you all on your achievements over the last 25 years and value the true friendships formed with you and numerous fellow fans who we would never had met had it not been for Longdogs. Finally best wishes especially to Vaughan and Gwen Pearce for a long, happy and healthy retirement and to Vicky Whitlock for grasping the management baton and running with it.

Show of Hands and Longdogs changed our lives in so many ways. It's all your fault guys, but to quote the 70's prog rock band Caravan, "if I could do it all over again I'd do it all over you" :)

Dave & Dee Brotherton (St Ives Festival):

For the past 12 years or so we have been privileged to work with Show of Hands and their crew and have never been disappointed by their professionalism and enthusiasm to deliver an outstanding show. We love how an empty venue at lunchtime slowly starts to get atmosphere as the crew rig the PA and lighting and then as the afternoon progresses, Steve is usually first to arrive, and we catch up on things, talk through the format of the evening, followed by Miranda, with Phil usually last to arrive! The venue then really comes alive at sound check and then the audience - always a sell out - starts to arrive and we have a spectacular show with many, many wonderful comments from seasoned 'Longdogs' and newcomers alike. It's a real joy to work with such dedicated, talented and hard working musicians. Congratulations on 25 wonderful years, a real achievement'.

Jim Causley:

I think my first proper meeting with Show of Hands was back when I shared a house in Exeter with Jackie Oates and Matt Norman, and Jackie invited us to appear on her second album which she was recording with Phil in the Riverside Studios. After this initial meeting Phil got me to play on Mick Groves (of The Spinners fame) new solo album and Jackie and I also were invited to appear on Phil Beer's 'Box Set One'. Which reminds me; when's 'Box Set Two' coming out Phil?!

Shortly after this time I began performing with Essex boyband Mawkin as Mawkin:Causley and as we have all "witnessed" with many fortunate young acts, Steve and Phil are true ambassadors for new performers and were ever so encouraging to us during this early time; giving us advice, shout-outs, spreading the word and even introducing us as special guests and friends of SoH in their patrons concerts at Sidmouth, Trowbridge and Abbotsbury festivals. This was a huge leg-up for us all at the time and I think I speak for all when I say we are eternally grateful for this generous help and encouragement. And as if all that wasn't enough, they invited us to make a cameo on their latest boundary-breaking album 'Arrogance, Ignorance and Greed' which was a real thrill. I was especially excited that I was chosen to be the voice of a scavenging East Devon wrecker in 'The Napoli'. It's quite nice to be type-cast now and then!

Since then I have guested on several Show of Hands albums and Steve also invited me to be the opening act for his 2011 solo tour, which as well as being a massive treat and an honour, was a real education and apprenticeship in the skill of performing and entertaining an audience, as well as the discipline and hard slog of solo touring for several weeks on end. The sheer professionalism that Steve and Phil exude is a great lesson for any aspiring performer. Show of Hands continue to be a great inspiration for me and I consider myself very lucky to count them as friends and to share the same gorgeous and unique West Country home. (I mean we live in the same county, we don't actually share a house, that would be too far!) Last year I recorded my first album of entirely self-penned material, greatly encouraged by producers Phil and SoH's beloved Mark Tucker and I was very blessed to have as guests on my album, not only Steve, Phil and Miranda, but nearly all of our shared friends in common (Rex Preston, Seth & Sean Lakeman, Kathryn Roberts, Phil Henry & Hannah Martin, The Claque, Jackie Oates, Matt Norman, Nick Wyke & Becki Driscoll, Ninebarrow, James Dumbelton, The Dartmoor Pixie Band, Lukas Drinkwater...) from the West Country folk scene which reminds me how overly fortunate we are in this part of the world when it comes to musical talent, especially in the folk and roots music scene. Many of these people I met through Show of Hands and I see them as the thread which binds us all together and the flag-bearers who have taken their pride in our wonderful Wild West far beyond this region, throughout Britain and the world!

Peter Chegwyn:

Many of Phil & Steve's early gigs were in backstreet bars in Gosport, Hampshire. In Olivers Bar the audience showed their appreciation after each song, not by applauding but by shouting out items of furniture... 'Sideboard', 'Chest of Drawers', 'Chaise Longue' etc. If you listen closely to the CD of the first Royal Albert Hall concert in 1996 you can just hear a 'Sideboard' among the applause at the end of 'The Galway Farmer'.

Phil & Steve sometimes stayed in a small Gosport guest house. If feeling hungry after a gig they would walk to Gosport's only all-night burger bar, The Night Owl, where Terry the proprietor would give them a free burger and chips in return for a swift music lesson on whichever instrument he was learning to play at the time. More than one passing drunk couldn't believe their eyes when seeing Phil teaching the guitar in the middle of the main A32 Forton Road at around 2 in the morning.

Show of Hands first played the Gosport Festival in 1992, drawing twice as many people as a young band who performed a few nights later. That band was called Take That. Wonder what happened to them?

Steve Heap

When Steve and Phil first got together I heard on the grapevine that they were doing this and would call themselves Show of Hands. I thought at the time, and I think I may have even told Phil, that I thought it was a silly name. Just shows how much I know!

Phil played Towersey and for some strange reason left his guitar behind. It sat in our office being played by a variety of visitors for several months before finally being returned to him at Folk by the Oak festival day. He didn't seem to miss it, but nevertheless was delighted to get it back.

And finally-

Steve and Phil dropped into my office when we were in Aylesbury, Buckinghamshire one day and to cut a long story short said 'Would you like to promote us to celebrate our first five years together at the Royal Albert Hall?' We took it on and Mrs Casey Music was proud to be the producers of their first Royal Albert Hall sell-out gig. I think that was the one where Steve asked his then girlfriend to marry him, from main stage in the middle of a concert.

I remember the concert started just a few minutes late because as I was about to go to stage and introduce the band one of the amps blew up and the PA crew were seen chasing around making last minute repairs. The audience probably didn't notice but it did lead to a bit of nail-biting in the green room.

As we all know the concert was a great success.

Do give my best wishes to the boys. They have done great things for the folk and roots music scene in song writing, presentation, media coverage and an amazing ambassador role, hoping to draw a new audience into our concerts and festivals. If we were giving out gongs they would be top of my list.

Philip Henry and Hannah Martin:

It was back in 2009 that Steve spotted us busking on Sidmouth sea front during folk week. We were regulars there then, living in an isolated Devonian caravan, and touring round the festival circuit with alt-folk band The Roots Union. We were thrilled when Steve introduced himself and made enthusiastic noises about our music. We were bowled over when he offered to get us in to the sold out Show of Hands gig that evening - but later that afternoon we decided he had probably just said it casually, would have plenty of other things to be thinking about, and wouldn't remember us. We didn't want to hassle him, so we didn't go along. It was very embarrassing when we bumped into him the next day, and he said, "Where were you?! I waited by the gate to get you in to the gig!". But luckily, despite learning the embarrassing way that Steve is a man of his word, we didn't offend him too badly! In fact, shortly after this, Phil and Steve invited us to support them on a string of dates. They both also took us on the road as support for their solo shows, each of them deliberately introducing us to their contacts, promoters, and audience, and launching our career on to a whole new level. It felt a bit like fairy godfathers were waving their wands (although I'm not sure how thrilled they'd be with that description. Once, at a support slot for Steve, I unintentionally managed to imply he was wearing ladies tights under his trousers. He wasn't thrilled then either!)

When we started playing as a duo, we had a five year plan, to make a living through playing music. Those five years concluded, almost to the day, with us winning the award for Best Duo at the 2014 BBC Radio Two Folk Awards. It was so fitting that Phil and Steve were the ones to present it to us. Not just great musicians - but generous dispensers of advice, lenders of equipment, and champion supporters of so many other music makers too. They have carved out the path for the independent musicians of today, and we're very lucky to be able to follow them down it. Huge thanks, always, to them both - and here's to their next 25 years!

Megan Henwood:

I have learnt a great deal from watching Show of Hands play and the kindness and belief they have shown me has been incredible. They have an inspiring approach to the scene around them, they work hard with open minds and a deep professionalism. In an industry that is an ever changing beast, to withhold a loyal fan base spanning over 3 decades and keep the music at the forefront is no mean feat. On top of that, throughout their journey they have been so generous with their support and guidance to emerging artists like myself. Wonderful men.

Simon Mayo:

You've got the albums, you've seen the gigs, now read the book!

Two of the sexiest folk singers you'll ever meet. Now with pictures!

Harmonies, history and truth

There isn't a bedside table in the land that wouldn't be improved with one of these beauties sitting on top it (I mean the book, not Steve or Phil. Though they'd be good at that too).

Jackie Oates:

Phil and Steve have been invaluable for me and most certainly, without their time and energy, I wouldn't have been able to sustain a career in the folk world.

I first met Phil during the Winter of 2004 when I had just graduated and was a little bit lost and searching for some inspiration and direction. He very kindly agreed to spend a day recording an EP at his studio in Countess Wear. I nervously put together a very over ambitious set of songs with my friend Martin Keates who came over from Manchester specially. The day arrived and went very quickly and in typical style we only scratched the surface! My EP haphazardly morphed into a full length album featuring all manner of musicians from the Devon folk scene, and many, many weekends of recording and re-recording. It was released in 2006, and I was delighted to receive some very kind reviews, airplay and a folk award nomination. I supported Phil on a solo tour the following year and played at the Royal Albert Hall as part of a string trio. We then made the 'Violet Hour' which was released in 2008 and for this I picked up the Horizon and Best Traditional Track Awards at the Folk Awards. I supported Show of Hands on their Spires and Beams Tour in 2010 and have duetted with Steve on the Keys of Canterbury and The Vale (Arrogance, Ignorance and Greed), various tracks on 'Centenary' and most recently Mesopotamia and Hambledon Fair (The Long Way Home). I've always seen my little moments of music making with Show of Hands as moments that my younger self would not have believed I'd ever have been fortunate enough to experience. My brother, my Dad and me were appreciative audience members throughout my high school years. I am very lucky to have been one of the young musicians who had this opportunity and I continue to be inspired and nourished by our friendship. *Jackie xxx*

Gerard O'Farrell:

Show of Hands has always been a fascinating balance between 'wanting to be a star', and 'wanting to be with my friends'.

Some of the biggest moments have involved people who really have nothing to do with music at all, but the size of the performance from essentially just 2 guys on a village hall stage has convinced, thrilled, empowered those and thousands of others. The decision to focus on the journey and not the result has always kept Show of Hands down to earth, but why not make the journey exciting! India, The Royal Albert Hall, Folk Album of the Year, Folk Artist of the Year .... all thrilling stuff, and to bring your friends too - unbelievably rewarding! There is more to come I am sure - 1996 to now, who knows, maybe the internet has turned into possibly the biggest Village Hall ever...

Mark Radcliffe:

When, every year, it comes round to Young Folk Award time on Radio 2, I'm always sure to remind my colleagues that as well as truly gifted musicians, we have to make sure we reward and encourage the songwriters.

Musicianship is something to be massively valued but unless someone keeps coming up with great songs for them to play we get into ever decreasing circles. Show of Hands then, it stands to reason, have the perfect balance. A sickeningly talented and sensitive player of a bewildering array of instruments in Phil, and a limitless supply of thought-provoking, heartfelt songs from Steve. I think folk music has to tell the stories of the working man and woman in the world we live in and confront some of the burning issues of the day. Steve is a master of this and is especially good at rooting his work in the landscape he knows so well. Once Phil adds his mastery, the picture is complete. They're both bloody good singers too – particularly when their honorary third member Miranda joins them in that perfect three part harmony. Their ability to fill a stage and hold a huge crowd in rapt attention is a wonder to behold, especially as it's achieved with only a few simple acoustic instruments. Of course I don't want this to be too much of a glowing eulogy as they're bigheads already. I could tell you about the time Steve appeared in full Scottish costume on stage at the Royal Concert Hall in Glasgow singing Caledonia, only to be told afterwards that he'd got the kilt on backwards, but I won't. I could also tell you about the time that Phil couldn't be bothered coming to the prestigious Radio 2 Folk Awards as he was busy draining the bilges of his boat, but I won't. However I enjoy their company a lot and will never forget the memorable day they joined me on air live from a Devon pub so I was able to say that I was 'taking beer with Phil Beer in Beer'. Ask Steve to repeat this story and it will inevitably include the worst Mark Radcliffe impression you are ever likely to hear. Show of Hands though, there's no-one else like them and long may they reign.
Mark Radcliffe, Dirty Old Town, 6/2/17

Steve Sheldon:

My first contact with Phil & Steve came at a small folk club that I ran in Surrey in the late 1970s. Phil was booked along with his then musical partner, Paul Downes, and it was they who recommended that I should book Paul's brother, Warwick, who was in a duo with Steve. Chatting with Steve after the gig, he mentioned his idea for forming a group and calling it Show of Hands. Over a decade went by before I saw the incarnation of this idea and it wasn't all plain sailing. The second gig my wife and I saw them at was in Brentwood in Essex. There were nine people and a dog (really) in the audience at the start of the night, although it did later swell to twenty two. When they did "Exile" someone in the "crowd" provided an impromptu flute accompaniment; an event I still have on cassette somewhere. During the early years the material wasn't exclusively self-penned or traditional. At various times we heard "Honky Tonk Women", Bowie's "Starman" and, on one memorable occasion, the old Joe Loss favourite, "Wheels".

In 1997 Phil and Steve did a birthday gig in France for some friends of ours who lived there. As the audience was going to be a mixture of French and British, our friends printed translations of some of the songs, so that the French would have some idea what was going on. When it came to "The Galway Farmer" Steve asked Phil to read out the translation as they went along. Phil coped reasonably well until they discovered that they only had half the translation. Suggestions from the audience began to add to the chaos and by the time Steve got to the line "I cursed my farmer's luck to hell" the plot was on its way south without a compass. Phil looked round hopefully and cried "Merde! Je suis infirmière", which he thought meant "Sh*t, I am a farmer." Both Brits and French collapsed with laughter, some struggling to catch their breath. It later transpired that the French were overcome by Phil's declaration that he was a nurse!

Over the years we've been privileged to occasionally oil the wheels of their career, to the extent that we're proud to call them friends. What's most impressive is the way they have adapted as they've become a bigger act. The audience at the first Albert Hall gig was more nervous on their behalf than they were themselves. That confidence, that first became evident to many after the Ralph McTell tour, has driven them to perform some of the best gigs I've seen over the last 25 years, whether in pubs, village halls, arts' centres, festivals or major venues. From The Bull in Bridport to their first Cropredy festival and through the various Albert Hall concerts, Eden Project gigs and the Shrouds of the Somme at Exeter Cathedral, they have never disappointed.

Alan and Sandra Surtees (Shrewsbury Festival,):

"Well Shrewsbury Folk Festival wouldn't be complete without the especially constructed "Mr Knightley's Compound" where our patron has his own back stage camping area for himself and selected guests; an area where the nights are very long".

Will Thomas (former Show of Hands crew member):

I am forever thankful and mindful of the work and the touring that I got to do with Phil and Steve. We got to see our own country in a way that very few of my contemporaries do. If anything, that's the most important thing I have taken from my time with Show of Hands.

Vicky Whitlock:

Vicky Whitlock - the epitome of a 'dragee', taken along to a Show of Hands gig in the early 1990's by her Dad, Broadstairs Folk Festival I think. I bought all of their CDs to date and signed up for the infamous mailing list. As a result my friends and I went to see Phil and Steve at a tiny pub called the Who'd a Thought It on Dartmoor, and I have followed them ever since. Phil called me up one day to ask about a venue that had rung and asked to book them (I forget which now), and I was able to tell him that the Oyster Band had played there not long before, so it should be pretty good for them, and it was! I stayed in touch with Phil over the years, catching the band at gigs. In 2009 Phil asked me to look after his bookings and record label Chudleigh Roots, which I blended with my own marketing consultancy business. In 2012, along with my business partner, Amanda Howland in Firebrand Music, I took on the bookings for Steve's Grow Your Own Gig concept - receiving over 750 enquiries for a tour of just 70 gigs. Since then we have been proud to take on Show of Hands and take forward those ideas set out by Gerard.

INDEX OF PHOTOGRAPHERS

COVER DESIGN BY STYLOROUGE MAIN PHOTOGRAPH BY BERND OTT
Photographs credited relative to their position on the page; left to right, then top to bottom unless stated otherwise. Initials refer to the key above.
Pg.4: JBE Pg.5: MCA Pg.6: NP, SKA, PBA (1996), BW (2007), IB (2008), JT Pg.7: JDO (2007), JDO (2007), JDO (2007), SOHA (2004), SOHA (2004), SW (2001), ROC (2016), JDO (2007), BW (2007), IB (2008), SW (2001), JDO (2007), SOHA (2004), SOHA (2003), FM (2009), BW (2007) Pg.8: SW (2001), BW (2007), SS (2001), BW (2007), PH (2012) Pg.9: SW (2001), SW (2001), JDO (2007), SW (2001), SOHA (1996), JDO (2007), SW (2001), CB (2001), SW (2001), SW (2001), JDO (2007), SW (2001), SKA (1996), L (2012), L (2012), MSA (2007), BW (2007), SW (2001) Pg.11: SW (2001) Pg.12: All PH (2012) Pg.13: All PH (2012) except Miranda, L (2012) Pg.14: All PH (2012) Pgs.16-17: BW Pg.18: SKA, PBA, PBA Pg.19: All PBA Pg.20: Left, both PBA, right JB Pg.21: Top PBA, bottom SKA Pg.22: SOHA Pg.23: PBA Pgs.24-25: All SKA Pg.27: Left, SKA, right PBA Pg.28: PBA, SKA Pg.29: ROC, SKA, PBA, SKA Pg.30: All ROC, except centre, PE Pg.31: All ROC Pg.32: BMC Pg.33: Left, BD, right, ROC Pg.34: PBA, SKA Pg.35: JB, JS, JB, all rest PBA Pg.36: ROC, SOHA, SKA, ROC, RM Pg.37: collage, all ROC, PBA Pg.38: Both JB Pg.39: SW Pg.40: JBE, PBA Pg.41: JB, RB Pg.42: EM Pg.43: ROC, IN, NP, PBA Pg.44: NP, all rest SKA Pg.45: ROC, ROC, NP Pg.46: ROC Pg.47: ROC, JT, ROC Pg.48: ROC Pg.49: ROC, JB Pg.50: ROC, NI Pg.51: All top, NI, SW, ROC Pgs.52-53: All ROC Pg.54: MCA Pgs.56-57: ROC Pg.58: EM Pg.59: GW, SW (2001), JT Pg.60: ROC, SKA, PG, ROC Pg.61: SKA, JB, SOHA Pg.62: Left, SKA, PBA, CB, SS, right, NP Pg.63: GW Pg.64: All left, ROC, right SKA Pg.65: BW, ROC Pg.66: NI Pg.67: tl ROC, bl NI, right, t-b, GOF, ROC, SOHA Pg.68: NP, JBE, JBE Pg.69: JA Pg.70: All PBA Pg.71: All JB Pg.73: ROC, VGP Pg.74: JBE, PBA Pgs.75-76: SW Pg.77: All SOHA Pg.79: VGP, MSA Pg.80: CLIC, SOHA Pg.81: Left, t-b, IB, MSA, right t-b, VGP, NP, SOHA Pgs.82-83: MW Pg.85: MSA, IB (2008), JT (2008) Pg.86: JW Pg.87: ROC, D Pg.88: JBE, SOHA, EM Pgs.89-90: All ROC Pg.91: SOHA, JAN, JAN, CB Pg.92: MT Pg.93: MT, right t-b, VGP, SOHA Pg.94: NP & SS (multiple), br MSA Pg.95: ROC Pg.96: MT, SOHA Pg.97: GW, NI Pg.99: top ROC, all rest SOHA Pg.100: PBE Pg.101: JT (2000) Pg.102: NT/GN Pg.103: BO Pgs.104-105: COH/ROC Pgs.106-107: All B&W shots, BO, all colour shots, ROC Pg.108: PBA, SOHA Pg.109: ROC Pg.110: SOHA (2007), SS (2001), SOHA, DK (2007) Pg.111: Both MSA Pg.112: TW Pg.113: ROC Pg.114: ROC, MW Pg.115: MT Pg.117: MT Pg.118: BW, MA Pg.119: Left, MA, right, MT, SOHA, ROC Pg.120: CB Pg.121: JA (2005) Pgs.122-123: JC Pg.124: All SOHA Pg.125: JC Pg.126: JT Pg.127: JT, TW, SOHA Pg.130: ROC Pgs.134-135: ROC Pg.136: IB, SC, SBA Pg.137: Both ROC Pg.139: All ROC Pg.140: JT, AB, JT Pg.141: BW, HW Pg.142: BW, PBA, ROC Pg.143: Left t-b, BL, SOHA, right, all BL Pg.144: MR Pg.145: left MR, right SKA Pgs.146-147: ROC Pg.148: BO Pg.149: All top, ROC, bottom, AB Pg.150: DT/AG, MA, DT/AG, ROC Pg.151: DT/AG Pg.152: ROC Pg.153: ROC, GD Pgs.154-155: All ROC Pg.156: MA Pg.157: MR Pgs.158-159: All ROC Pg.160: Both SOHA Pg.161: top SBA, bottom KH, ROC Pg.162: ROC Pg.163: ROC, MC, ROC, BW, BW Pg.164: AL, ROC Pg.165: ROC Pg.166: SKA, ROC, SOHA, SOHA, PBA Pg.167: MW (2004) Pg.168: SKA, PBA Pg.169: PBA Pg.170: Left t-b, SOHA, SOHA, MAI, right large GD, inset, C Pg.171: MT, BM, BW Pgs.172-173: VGP Pg.174: Left, t-b, VGP, JT, JT, SOHA, right MC Pg.175: JT, PH, IB, SOHA Pg.176: PH Pg.177: ROC Pg.178: CB Pg.179: CB, DM, SOHA Pg.180: ROC Pg.181: t-b PBA, EOC, PH, SOHA Pgs.182-183: SOHA (2008) Pg.184: JT (2002) Pg.185: clockwise from bl, FM (2010), HW (2015), FM (2010), FM (2010), FM (2009), FM (2010), FM (2010), FM (2010), SS (1999), FM (2010), HW (2015), SS (2002), FM (2010), FM (2010). Centre, AT (2016), below centre, HW (2015) Pg.186: NP (2014), FM (2010), NP (2001), PBA (2006), AT (2016), FM (2010), PBA (2016), FM (2010), FM (2010), SOHA (2011) Pg.187: clockwise from tl, HW (2015), FM (2010), SOHA, FM (2010), SOHA (2011), FM (2010), PBA (2016), HW (2015), FM (2010), PBA (2016), FM (2010). Centre, SOHA (2011). Below centre, l-r, FM (2010), FM (2010), SOHA (2005), SOHA (2011) Pg.188: SOHA, MN, PBA Pg.189: Left, both, PBA, right t-b, JAN, VGP, SKA Pg.190: AB, BW, CJ, SKA, ROC, SOHA (2003), FM (2009) Pg.191: PBA, NP, NP, SS, PBA Pg.192: SKA Pg.193: SKA, NP, CK Pg.195: TW Pg.196: SOHA, EMM Pg.197: Left t-b, ROC, TW (2016), SC, IB (2008), HW (2015), EOC, centre t-b, MS, HW (2015), DM (2011), BW, SOHA (2007), MW (2004), right t-b, MW (2004), VGP (2006), IEC, SOHA (2011), MAI (2012). Top right, PBA (2007) Pg.198: Top left, SKA, all others SB, except large lower centre, BBC Pg.199: All SB Pgs.200-201: Both ROC Pg.202: TW, SB Pg.203: Centre, t-b, SKA, SKA, SKA, SOHA, SOHA, CK Pgs.204-205: ROC Pgs.206-207: All TW (2016) Pg.208: AL (2012) Pg.209: JDO (2007), BW (2007), bg MR Pg.210: ROC Pg.211: TB, VGP (2006) Pgs.212-3: TW (2016) Pg.222: LMB
Although every effort has been made to credit copyright holders and seek permission, this hasn't always been possible.
If you have not been credited and wish to be at reprint, then please get in contact with Flood Gallery Publishing.